LIFE
IN THE
RIGHT
SEAT

TINA COONCE

LIFE IN THE RIGHT SEAT
Copyright © 2005 by Tina Coonce

Published by
TCT MINISTRIES, INC.
P.O BOX 1010
MARION, IL 62959

Printed in the United States of America.

DEDICATION

*This book is dedicated to those who
have offered me unending encouragement
and support through the myriad trials of life.
Some have remained loving and patient in spite
of innumerable challenges, such as my beautiful
daughters, Victoria Clark and Julie Coonce-Nolan,
my faithful sister, Dr. Mary Ellen Bogard, and
my God-given friend, Nancy Starkweather.
I am grateful to them all, including the
TCT partners, whose payers and
support made the story possible.*

CONTENTS

INTRODUCTION

In any airplane cockpit, the Pilot-in-Command is the one in control. According to Federal Aviation Authority regulations, he (or she) has ultimate responsibility for everything connected to the flight, including the safety of the passengers and the craft itself.

Sometimes, however, the Pilot-in-Command is not alone. A co-pilot is seated to his right. In fact, many airplanes are so complex a second person is necessary to perform functions from the right seat. That individual must be fully knowledgeable and capable of fulfilling the pilot's role if necessary. In the event of an emergency or even an unforeseen tragedy—such as the death of the Pilot-in-Command—the person in the right seat must be qualified to handle the situation with complete competence. He is fully prepared and undergoes as much training, testing, and continuing instruction as the Pilot-in-Command. Still, he's not in charge during the going-as-planned, day-to-day flights. His job resides in the right seat.

MY SPECIAL PLACE

I know the right seat well.

In 1977 my husband, Garth, and I founded TCT Ministries, a worldwide Christian television network. Early in our outreach, Garth gave his testimony at a Full

Gospel Business Men's Fellowship International (FGBMFI) meeting.

A precious man named Bill Allen was touched by what he heard and, after the service, offered Garth a wonderful donation: an old Cessna 310, a twin-engine airplane.

Bill was an electrical contractor who had been in aviation for years and still owned several aircraft. Soon to retire, he saw the need of two young eager television pioneers and, led by the Holy Spirit, chose to help our ministry. The thrill of receiving such a generous gift was almost overwhelming.

At that time, we lived in Cincinnati, Ohio, and had two stations, both a six-hour drive in opposite directions from our home—one in Marion, Illinois, and the other in Saginaw, Michigan.

We spent countless hours driving between those sites—in a van— attending to the tasks of the fledgling ministry. Those early days were exciting (after all, we were working for the Lord!), but they were exhausting. The airplane would minimize our travel time and maximize our resources so we could focus on more important matters—like the growth of the network!

TIME TO FLY

My husband, as you will learn in this book, is an extraordinary man! When he decides to do something, he doesn't let anything stand in his way.

Usually it takes an aspiring pilot a full year to earn a pilot's license, but Garth finished in three months. I was so busy doing much of the office work I didn't see how I could ever find the time to start working on my own license. Garth, however, knew the importance. One day he simply made the appointment for me with an instructor, informed me I *was* going—and I showed up as scheduled.

Nearly 30 years and 18 television stations later, Garth is still the Pilot-in-Command, and I am there beside him, in the right seat.

ASSISTING, ADVISING, ENCOURAGING

My place beside my husband isn't confined to our hours in flight. With TCT, Garth is in charge, but I'm next to him almost every step of the way, trying to help fulfill his vision—assisting, advising and encouraging him. And, to be honest, sometimes *frustrating* him. But guess what: he likes having me by his side!

The same holds true in our marriage. Garth is the head of the household and the main decision maker. I still assist, advise, encourage—and sometimes frustrate him in our personal life. Of course, like any wife, there are some aspects of our daily lives that I oversee, but, overall, I'm second in command. Neither of us would have it any other way.

Sadly, many today—men and women alike—think it's better to be in charge. Why would anyone voluntarily choose to sit in the right seat? For me the answer comes easy: it's God's will.

As you will learn on these pages, I can't say I always took my place in the right seat without some resistance, either in the ministry or my marriage. However, I hope

9

you will see in this story and in the lessons I have learned, God's way is always the best. The Almighty reminds us, *"For My thoughts are not your thoughts, nor are your ways My ways...For as the heavens are higher than the earth, so are My ways higher than your ways"* (Isaiah 55:8–9).

God's Plan for You

The passion I had for the Bible as a young Christian is still strong. Allowing the Word to be sown in me has been the foundation of my life—as a child of God, a woman, a ministry partner and a wife.

Through the Scripture, I've learned that God has wondrous plans for me and you. He is such a loving Father and He only desires what is best for us. Yet, we sometimes struggle with convincing our hearts of His knowledge and wisdom. Often, we stubbornly want to run our lives on our own terms.

This is why spending time in the Word is so vital. It keeps our focus on God rather than on ourselves and, like a mirror, reveals the true condition of our lives.

What follows are lessons on how I've submitted to God and taken my place in the right seat—in the air, in my ministry and in my marriage.

I fully realize the Lord's plan for me is not His plan for you, but I trust He will use these teachings and my personal stories to reveal aspects of your own life in which He desires to work.

Chapter 1

A Bumpy Road

As I sit down to write what led me to find my place in "the right seat," I can't help but think, "Who wants to read about me? I'm just an ordinary person."

Then I realize a life submitted to Christ and touched by Him is *never* ordinary. The moment we choose to follow the Lord, we enter the realm of the extraordinary. He takes our lives and transforms us by teaching, loving and making us more like Himself. Once we say "Yes," to the Lord, anything is possible.

Perhaps my earliest memory is my decision for Christ when I was just four years old. A neighbor woman took my mother and me to a revival meeting at a Nazarene church. Though my young mind didn't grasp or comprehend much, I knew without any doubt I wanted to obey Jesus and I responded to the altar call with deep sobs of contrition.

I believe the decision was real in my heart, yet, sadly, there wasn't anyone or anything to nurture my young faith. Yet, God saw me, and eventually worked things out according to His divine plan.

At four years old, none of us has much knowledge, but I believe my spirit responded to the voice of the Holy Spirit that night and I made a genuine decision to follow the Lord. After all, Jesus Himself said, *"Let the children alone, and do not hinder them from coming to Me; for the kingdom of heaven belongs to such as these"* (Matthew 19:14).

Even at this tender age, I knew God was *good,* and I needed Him.

It's a miracle I even attended church that night. You see, ours was not a godly home. Mother rarely accompanied us to a house of worship, instead we were sent.

I'm sure there were people praying for us—possibly neighbors or relatives, perhaps those I had never met. I fully believe their prayers led me to salvation.

ON THE MOVE

Our parents did the best they could as they struggled through life without a real knowledge of God's love.

My mother, Hazel, was an uneducated simple country girl who married Wayne "Jack" Robbins at the age of 18. He was a skilled mechanic and heavy equipment operator, working for Morrison-Knudson, one of the world's major construction companies of that era. They were building dams and bridges all over the western states.

Because of his occupation, we moved constantly from state to state during my childhood.

THE OREGON TRAIL.

My mother's heritage is an ethnic mix. She had a grandmother who claimed to be a gypsy with a background in fortune telling. On her side, I also have a Spanish Catholic legacy.

In my genealogy search I learned how one of my ancestors left Virginia as a young girl and headed west with her family on the Oregon Trail.

When they reached the rapids of the Columbia River, both the covered wagons and people had to be portaged around in various ways. The family sent the young girl over the mountain with an Indian on horseback. He promised he wouldn't hurt the "little white squaw" if they gave him a red blanket. It was a colorful story I will always remember.

Their journey began with a half-dozen wagons, several fine teams, loose horses, milk cows and stock cattle. When they arrived in Oregon City, they were driving a milk cow and a mule. All the horses had died, and all the wagons, except one, were left along the way.

The girl eventually grew up and married a romantic young man who had emigrated from Scotland—a story straight out of the movies. The descendants of this couple helped populate the state of Oregon.

I was fascinated to learn how they purchased a piece of property, but the wife, thinking it wasn't a good investment, traded it for a horse. Today, that piece of land is part of downtown Portland!

My genealogy research also uncovered distant relatives who were ministers of the Gospel. I believe they prayed for me and God honored those prayers. His hand is at work on our behalf even when we don't know or see it. We may never fully understand until we step into eternity.

DAD'S INDIAN HERITAGE

My father, however, remains a mystery I have never been able to solve. As best I can determine, he was the son of an Indian on the west coast. Born around 1905, he was intelligent and capable, yet uneducated.

In those days, the standards of child rearing were often brutal. Most lived in poverty—desperate to survive the best they could, not overly concerned about what was legal or moral.

When my parents were first married, my dad told my mother the story of how his Indian mother returned to the reservation and was fatally injured while trying to pull a cow out of the mud!

My grandfather then remarried—to a "wicked step

mother" who was unkind to the children. They had a large house on a hill in Oakland, California. One of the tidbits I gleaned was that, for some unknown reason, my grandfather brought his new wife roses every day!

A CHECKERED PAST

My mother married my birth father when she was 18 years old. She later learned her own parents (mother and step-father) had forced the union because my father had taken her over the state line to find work in the Sierra Nevada mountains. They threatened to prosecute him with the Mann Act if he didn't marry her. (The Mann Act, passed in 1910, made it a federal offense to transport individuals under the age of 18 across state lines to engage in sexual activity. The intent was to regulate interstate prostitution, not to apply to personal escapades.)

My mother had no idea of his true background until a few years later, when he was sent to jail in Quincy, California, for writing bad checks. The officials also found out through his fingerprints he had an assumed identity. Mother was told he had served a year and a half at San Quentin prison for robbery.

The legal authorities gave her his real name and all the sordid details. She had the records, but at the time didn't know how to deal with such issues. Eventually, the papers were lost and she just went on with life.

My father was an alcoholic, yet an extremely hard-working man in heavy construction.

We were always existing at the lower socioeconomic level and, because of the constant moving, never really adapted to communities around us.

The Issue of Identity

Since I grew up without much of an identity, I didn't have one to overcome!

When I read the story of Abraham, I was intrigued by God telling him, "Come out of your father's house and go to a land I will show you. I will give you a new identity and a new relationship."

Some people resist change because they feel what they have is so good they don't want to leave their comfort zone.

In my case, it was easy for the Lord to make me into what He desired since I didn't have to fight to rid myself of something else. Regardless of our background, we need to yield to whatever the Father has in store. The Bible tells us to *"...present your bodies a living sacrifice, holy, acceptable unto God, which is your reasonable service"* (Romans 12:1 KJV).

When we accept Christ and allow Him to make the decisions for our future, He begins the process of stamping His image in us, causing us to become like Him.

We need to realize the difficulties He allows in our path are to accomplish His purpose. However, when most people face a problem they immediately forget the Lord and attempt to handle the situation themselves. In the process they make a disaster out of life.

Thank God, He is gracious and merciful. The Lord is patiently waiting to pick us up, dust us off, put us back on our feet and help us move forward.

We are like the children of Israel. How many times do we have to face the same mountain before we figure out the solution? It's time to die to self and allow the Spirit to take preeminence—instead of relying only on our soul and body.

UNCONNECTED?

The Bible says God knew us and placed us for a purpose before we were born. In His sovereignty and foreknowledge I am doing what He planned—not because I am talented or have a stellar background or education. It is because of what He has divinely ordered.

I believe two or three generations back there were believers in Christ who prayed for me before I even knew of them.

Both my mother and father were loners and the definition of "black sheep." As a result, close family relationships and identity did not exist for us.

My sister and I often laughed over the fact we were

just "molecules floating in space, unconnected to anything."

I truly believe that God meant for people to have knowledge of their identity. The children of Israel knew who they belonged to—they recognized their tribe and knew their place in Jewish society.

A TIME OF PREPARATION

Unfortunately, my father's alcoholic behavior often ended his work even before the jobs were finished. Because of his natural intelligence and skill level, he was more than once considered for choice international assignments, but his recognized failure to maintain a stable home for his family disqualified him for such responsible positions.

Constant moving and upheaval took its toll on all of us, yet I can now look back and see how God was uniquely preparing me for the future—first as a corporate wife, and then in Christian ministry. At a young age, the Lord taught me how to leave what is familiar and adapt to any new situation.

In the myriad places we lived, there was usually some kind of church nearby, where I would attend Sunday School, Vacation Bible School or take catechism classes. In the process, I was exposed to God's Word in a variety of churches. It is another example of my Heavenly

Father's wisdom. When I was just a child, He knew what I would need later in my life.

These experiences prepared me to appreciate many different denominations—something I would later value in an interdenominational Christian television ministry.

A CRY FOR CONNECTION

Even with the good Christian people who labored in the local churches we attended, life was never easy. I was always "the new kid" in town and felt different.

Because both my mother and father had come from disconnected families themselves, they had no concept of how to build, let alone maintain, a healthy home life. There was practically no family structure to take comfort in, and any newly acquired friends would soon be left behind in the next move.

Once, as a young girl, my mother said she felt sorry for me when she overheard me arguing with a little neighborhood friend. I had been proudly telling him I had cousins, and he snidely accused, "Well, they aren't *real* cousins. They're just somebody close to your family who you call cousins!"

I stomped my little foot and vehemently cried, "They are too real cousins!" Even as a child, I wanted to feel I had a connection.

FEAR AND EMBARRASSMENT

Through our developing years, my older sister suffered more than I did. I couldn't quite grasp that our life was as awful as it was, but she was older, wiser and understood more. She experienced the fear and embarrassment of an alcoholic family, never fitting in with normal people as we constantly uprooted to new communities.

I was just the "little kid" growing up, not fully realizing things were so dysfunctional in our family.

Our bumpy road left an indelible mark on my sister. Thank God, with her intelligence and drive to succeed, she became a psychologist. With the Lord's help, we all have the ability to rise above whatever life hands us.

SHE CLAIMED "DESERTION"

As are many alcoholics, my father was abusive when he drank, and my mother finally left him when I entered high school. In the previous years, our usual pattern was that my father would move first to begin a new job and find a place for the family to live. Then, a week or so later, we would load up the car with our meager belongings and follow him to the new location.

This time, when he left for the new position in another state, she filed for divorce, claiming desertion, so he wouldn't be called to stand before a judge.

For a considerable time afterward, my mother was tormented by the fear he would come back and kill her. Thank God, it didn't happen. Years later we found out he remarried rather quickly and went on with his work.

A FRESH START

Eventually my mother, an attractive woman, remarried—to Jimmy Gravel, a man in the U.S. Air Force.

Military people expect to be relocated often, but usually their families can go wherever they are stationed. So shortly after their marriage, it was an unpleasant surprise when my stepfather received orders to work in the Azores for a full year. Because the work was highly classified, our family could not go with him.

With her new husband going away for a year, my mother decided to move from Montana to California so we could be near her brother, who was also in the military. He was stationed at Hamilton Air Force Base, near the San Francisco Bay area. Hamilton Field was called the "Country Club of the Air Force" because of its beautiful setting in sunny Marin County.

CULTURE SHOCK

High school was not a happy experience for me since I didn't really feel I belonged. Most kids had grown up together in the same community, but I was new in town and felt excluded.

Also, because of our family background and lack of funds, we were really naive when it came to fashion or grooming. Yes, we were clean, but didn't have a clue when it came to fixing our hair with the style of the day or applying the proper makeup. Other teens spent extra time trying to look their best, however, we weren't that sophisticated.

Moving to the San Francisco Bay area was quite a culture shock.

During my high school years I was a lost soul—just trying to get along. I dated several young men but didn't really maintain relationships because of my poor self-image.

I had an insatiable quest for knowledge and I enjoyed learning, but my grades took a nose dive when I started smoking, playing hooky and doing all those crazy things kids do when they don't have anybody to rein them in or point them in the right direction.

My husband and I have, with God's help, tried to give our children the things I *didn't* have—a stable home life where they are taught and given character building activities. I know first hand how difficult it is to grow up in a home without such values. It causes a child to have questions trying to figure out who they are, what life is all about and where they fit in.

AT THE POOL

Even though my stepfather was stationed overseas, we had base privileges such as shopping and entertainment, as military families do. Hamilton Air Force Base was quite elegant and we enjoyed the swimming pool. It was there on a summer afternoon I met a handsome young airman, Garth Coonce, who was also stationed at Hamilton. I was only 16, and Garth was four years older.

As he tells his friends, "She jumped on me in the water!"

I have to admit I did, although it was quite unintentional. I was just a careless teenager jumping happily into the pool without looking. (To his credit, he has been fixing my mistakes ever since!)

"ROSY THE RIVETTER"

Garth was born and raised in northeastern Ohio, and came from German, Swedish stock. His parents divorced when he was very young.

His mother made a living in the steel plants—as a "Rosy the Rivetter" factory worker. They lived with his grandmother and two bachelor uncles and there was no relationship with his father.

Growing up, his family didn't have much, so Garth

began working as a child to earn a little money to help with the expenses—delivering newspapers and mowing lawns in the days of the push mowers.

Early in life, Garth learned the value of hard work —that what you have is what you earn. In the process he understood a man's responsibility for taking care of his family—a character trait which continues to this day.

THE LOVE OF MY LIFE

Garth had enlisted in the military for four years because he was ready to see the world. After a stint in Iceland, he was now assigned to the electrical power production at Hamilton.

Regarding spiritual matters, he wasn't living for the Lord—and neither was I—yet he was a responsible, decent man. Sure, he was immature in some respects, yet there was a basic goodness inside him.

After dating for one year, Garth asked for my hand in marriage and I couldn't find any reason to say no. I had found the love of my life.

We announced our wedding date and reserved the chapel at Hamilton Air Force Base in San Rafael, California.

THE CHORUS GIRL!

Garth's family came out to the west coast from Ohio

for the event—and their first impression of me must have made them scratch their heads.

The night before we were to be married, I was in a stage production of the musical "Oklahoma!" I wasn't the star, just one of the chorus girls with stage makeup and a costume.

Since the director knew I was getting married the next morning, he told me I could leave a little early. So I was still wearing my stage outfit when I was introduced to Garth's family.

We had prearranged to meet them at a certain place and guide them the rest of the way into San Francisco.

It was a dark night and out of the car stepped his mother, stepfather and uncle. In the back sat his younger sister. I'll never forget the surprised look on her face when she peered out the window at this *hussy* with pancake makeup and a frilly costume from "Oklahoma!"

The next morning Garth and I were married.

"LET ME TAKE A PICTURE!"

The wedding my mother arranged for us was a modest affair. As a practical decision, I chose not to have a wedding dress because I wanted something I could wear on other occasions in the future. The thought of having a dress to be worn only once just didn't compute for me—every penny was too dear.

I selected a simple beige jacket dress. There were a few flowers, a small bouquet and I had an attendant, but the ceremony wasn't anything to write home about.

As we came out of the chapel, someone stopped Garth and me and said, "Let me take a picture!" There was no official photographer.

Several years later Garth's mother had it enlarged and colorized for us as a gift. It is such a wonderful memory.

PERFECT TIMING

Prior to our wedding, I lived with my mother in a small apartment. My sister was teaching school in Reno, Nevada.

At the time of our marriage, my stepfather's duty in the Azores was completed and he returned to the states, deciding to retire from the Air Force and join the technological world. He had a strong background in electronics and computers and helped to build the NORAD national defense facility in Cheyenne Mountain near Colorado Springs, Colorado.

His new job was with an electronics company in Philadelphia. My mother was excited about being reunited with him. After all, they were relatively newlyweds themselves!

The timing was absolutely perfect. My mother was leaving to join her husband and we would move into her apartment.

I quit my work as a theater usherette and stepped into my mother's job as an Avon representative. I took over her route, selling cosmetics door to door.

Originally, we planned to go to Hawaii on our honeymoon, but decided to do something practical instead. "Let's go east and take your mother with us," suggested Garth. "We'll take her to Pennsylvania and then go to Washington D.C. and see all the historic sites."

Not many people can say they took their mother with them on their honeymoon, but that's exactly what we did!

A WHIRLWIND TRIP

We first drove to Youngstown, Ohio, where Garth's family lived, and my mother took a bus the rest of the way to Philadelphia.

There was a wedding shower in our honor and we happily received much-needed items to set up housekeeping. These were certainly welcome since my mother had taken her few belongings with her.

Before the honeymoon trip, I was packing my clothes—shorts and halters and things a teenager might wear when my mom said, "Honey, you'd better pack something a little warmer than that!"

She was right! When we arrived in northeastern Ohio it was March—and we found ourselves in winter snow.

As part of the honeymoon adventure, we walked the sober fields at Gettysburg and toured our nation's capital. Then it was back to California where we lived for the next two years.

Preparing the Foundation

Garth worked the midnight shift at the power production unit on the base. Soon, however, he began a second job at a gas station so we could afford a better apartment. It wasn't great, but it was a small step up—and that's when I began to see the incredible potential he had.

I soon became pregnant and when Vicki arrived, Garth didn't want me to work. So, I took on the title of a stay-at-home mom while he continued to labor at the two jobs.

As a newly married young couple, we were happy, yet neither Garth nor I really understood each other. Even though Jesus was not at the heart of our marriage in those days, He worked in us, placing godly people in our path and preparing the foundation for a family and ministry.

HEADING EAST

Following Garth's stint in the service, he said, "I really think we should move back to Ohio." After all, it was his home.

I grew up in the west with wide expanses of clear blue skies and the magnificent Rocky Mountains. It was my vantage point of the world. To me, Ohio was like moving to another planet!

The three of us didn't have many material possessions, but we packed what we owned into a little trailer, hooked it up to our car and headed for a brand new adventure.

CHAPTER 2

A BRAND NEW WORLD

During my early-married years, I did my best to be a good wife and mother—to be thrifty and not wasteful.

I still smile when I think about the electric deep fryer we received as a wedding gift. I had used it a few times (not too successfully since I wasn't exactly a gourmet cook).

I kept the same old oil in the fryer and reused it over and over again. The thought of spending 25 cents to unnecessarily buy a new bottle of cooking oil was unthinkable to me.

When it came time to pack for the trip east, I just couldn't bear the thought of wasting the oil by pouring it out. Surely it could still be used when we reached Ohio! So I packed it very carefully in a way it could not be turned over and I secured the lid as best I could.

Miraculously, as that trailer bounced along behind

our car for 2,500 miles, only a few drops of the oil seeped out. I felt quite virtuous at having saved those pennies!

After we reached Youngstown, we stayed with Garth's mother while we were looking for an apartment of our own. In the meantime we stored our moving boxes temporarily in a relative's basement. Ironically, a fierce storm blew in the basement window and knocked some of the boxes over. I'm sure you can guess what finally spilled out!

The Old Saloon!

Moving to northeastern Ohio to be near Garth's family seemed like a good idea at the time. However, we had arrived in a dying industrial area.

This was a strange world to me, and I'm sure people considered me a "West Coast weirdo."

I wanted to talk about interesting topics like evolution, but couldn't find anybody who could or would—they were just interested in their day to day activites.

We lived with Garth's uncle for a year and a half in an old, dreadful house. It was like a family homestead, only without the charm! A hundred years earlier it had been built as a saloon out in the country. Eventually, a steel mill had been located right next to it.

The house was poorly constructed to begin with and through the years it had been expanded by unskilled workers. It was now in a terrible state of disrepair.

Those days were like being confined to a prison. It was a daily grind of hard work that never subsided. The steel mill next door was belching out a constant flood of graphite dust. It permeated the air and dirty film covered everything in the house—and I had a toddler!

Actually there were two uncles who lived there. The other was a truck driver who was in and out. Now I had three men and a little girl to take care of in a house which was physically impossible to keep clean.

THE DUNGEON

Monday was wash day and I'd work on the laundry all day long. At least there was an old washing machine with a wringer.

Trying to do the laundry in the basement was next to impossible. I felt I was taking my life in my hands every time I went down those rickety old steps into a hole in the ground which was more like a dungeon.

After putting the wash through the wringer, I hauled the wet baskets of clothes up the old steps that went outside through the storm cellar door. I'd hang them on the line and later in the day bring them inside. Of course, in the winter nothing really dried. It was grim.

I sprinkled the dried clothes with water from a pop bottle with holes punched in the top. Then I'd roll up the clothes, put them in a plastic bag and place them in the refrigerator. Don't ask me why, but this was the custom in those days.

Tuesday was ironing day—a chore which never seemed to end.

I can still see the grimy kitchen floor with it's ugly old green tile—with pieces chipped and broken. I'd spend hours on my hands and knees, scrubbing away with a Brillo pad, trying in vain to get the floor clean.

One day the preacher came to visit and as we talked, a mouse ran along the wall behind the couch. I was praying he wouldn't see it. On the window was an ugly torn shade I bought at a discount house for a quarter. It was just awful.

Garth worked at any odd job he could find, but times were tough. One day, I wanted to send a Father's Day card to my uncle, yet didn't have the money for a stamp.

As time progressed, we moved into other houses. They weren't upscale, but each one was a little improvement.

A NEW COMMITMENT

There would be other surprises in store—more profound ones.

Garth was raised in a Midwestern blue-collar industrial culture where women and children were expected to go to church, but most men didn't. He had made a commitment to Christ when he was 11 years old, but in his ensuing formative years, there were few male role models in his life for a boy to learn the qualities of spiritual manhood.

It was in Ohio God really went to work on me. I began visiting the Evangelical Congregational Church where Garth grew up. One of the first meetings I attended with his mother was a revival service and, at the age of 20, I recommitted my life to the Lord. I really believed things were going to be different—and they were.

I'll never forget the first time his mother took me to a "prayer meeting." I'd never been to a service by that name in my life.

As we were walking in the door I anxiously asked her, "Does everyone have to get on their knees, or have to pray out loud?"

Little did I know I would eventually be leading those weekly gatherings.

RICHES TO EXPLORE

From that point forward I had an insatiable desire for the Word of God. If you remember what it's like to be a babe in Christ, you know what I mean. Everything was so new and exciting. I had accepted Jesus, and now there was suddenly a whole new world to explore.

I could not absorb enough of the Bible and its unfathomable riches. Eagerly, I began to study and read everything I could get my hands on that would help me better understand Scripture.

I would borrow commentaries and reference books from pastors' libraries and spread them out on the dining room table. Whenever I got a chance, I'd run in and study, even if only for a few minutes.

Fortunately, I was blessed with a pastor who allowed me to ask him plenty of questions. He would point me to specific Scriptures, letting the Word of God speak to me, and it did—powerfully.

IN LOVE WITH THE WORD

By this time, our second daughter, Julie, was on her way. I was so consumed with the Scriptures I even took a Bible commentary with me to the hospital when I went into labor!

Garth and I have also experienced the heartache of premature births and loss of a child. Though our younger daughter Julie was a full-term healthy baby, the previous year we had lost a baby boy named Mark Thomas. Our first child, Vicki, had also been premature, but she survived after spending a month in an incubator in a military hospital.

TOTAL INVOLVEMENT

The Evangelical Church was similar to Baptist

theology. They preached the Word and taught it's importance for all of life's decisions.

In addition to my biblical studies, regular involvement in church activities was an important part of growing in Christian maturity. I happily sang in the choir and taught both children's and adult Sunday School classes. I eagerly helped with numerous other activities including Vacation Bible School, the Missionary Society, and I led the Youth Group.

If that was not enough, I was also elected "Class Leader"—the denomination's title for the individual who led the midweek prayer service.

NO ANSWER!

Every Sunday, we went to church, but as much as I wanted Garth to join us, he stayed home.

We were now living in an older two-story house and I figured out a way I could dial the phone downstairs and make it ring upstairs. On Sunday mornings as Garth was sleeping, I thought if I could wake him up, he would go to church. He soon caught on and didn't pick up the phone!

He had no problem with me attending the services, but it was obvious I wasn't supposed to make him do *anything*.

"WHAT ARE THEY DOING?"

After several years of studying Scripture, I was desperate for even more of the Lord.

I cherished the Word and my life in church, but there came a time when I felt I had learned everything I could from my current surroundings.

I prayed, "God, please help me find people who can teach me more about You."

He answered my prayer. Immediately, the Lord began to send individuals into my life who I respected—professional people who had their act together.

My curiosity concerning spiritual matters continued to grow.

After most Sunday evening services I'd take the girls to the Dairy Queen. On the way we would pass an Assembly of God church and noticed the service was still in progress. Then, after our ice cream treat, we'd drive back down the same street to find the meeting still in progress. Often, we could hear the singing and I wondered, "What on earth are those Pentecostals doing in there?"

THE CHARISMATIC MOVE

The time came when my passion for the things of

God grew beyond the walls of the church. I eagerly pursued more of the presence of the Lord in my life, devouring everything I could find about giants of the faith throughout history, as well as great churches and ministries in this present age.

Through regional inter-church activities and events, I began to meet new people and learn about something called the "baptism in the Holy Spirit."

These were the days of the Charismatic Move, as the Holy Spirit was poured out upon people in traditional churches all over the world. Along with so many others, I discovered what a profound difference the fullness of the Spirit makes in the walk of a believer—and in a church.

I knew Jesus, but now I was submitting my life to Him and allowing the Lord to have more of me.

Of course, the moment you are born again you become a temple of the Holy Spirit. But the baptism in the Holy Spirit opens up a new dimension in your spiritual life.

MY HEAVENLY ENCOUNTER

I still think about the night I received my personal Pentecostal experience, I was alone with the Lord and at one point prayed, "God, I am not coming out of this room until I receive the Baptism of the Holy Spirit!"

He graciously answered and for the next 45 minutes

I began to speak in a prayer language that was far too glorious to describe. I had never prayed so long in my life. But it wasn't me—the heavenly inspired words just flowed.

That same night, I was seated at our dining room table when Garth came in the door. He looked at me and he could see something had changed. "What happened to you?" he asked.

I couldn't even answer. I just sat there with a big grin on my face.

Later, when I tried to tell him what had taken place, Garth was sure I was crazy and was determined to prove me and my charismatic friends wrong! After all, he had grown up in church and had never heard anything about this "Holy Spirit" I was talking about. He simply could not relate.

Even though I had been saved, regenerated, and changed, loving the Word of God and doing everything I could for the Kingdom of God, the baptism in the Holy Spirit brought a powerful new dimension of His presence.

AN INDESCRIBABLE POWER

Now I knew first-hand what this baptism was all about.

When I began to spend time with people who functioned in the Spirit, I began to understand verses I didn't comprehend before.

Receiving the baptism of the Holy Spirit was a major turning point because it allowed God's fullness to come in a way it had never been.

Yes, the moment you are born again the Spirit resides within you and your body becomes a temple of the Holy Spirit. Yet, there is something about this God-ordained baptism that changes things.

I was in a church which was fiercely committed to the Word of God, the preaching of the Gospel and salvation. However, we literally did not know that people who walked in the fullness of the Spirit existed.

After my Pentecostal experience, I was careful not to push or force anything on my friends at church. I simply told them what happened to me, introduced them to other Spirit-filled believers and took them to meetings. It was just a natural response.

SHALLOW SAINTS?

Over the years, many Christians have made light of Charismatics—equating them with shallow, rather gullible people. My experience, however, was totally different. The Spirit-filled people I knew were accomplished, highly educated professionals who had a special relationship with the Lord. They had a value in society as well as in the Kingdom of God.

I met these people by reaching outside the four walls

of my church. They were leaders of women's prayer meetings and active in Christian women's clubs.

It was so exciting being around those who were absolutely in love with God and longed to be in His presence. Many of these Spirit-filled believers began worshiping at our church.

Unfortunately, leaders of the denomination told the pastor not to allow a Charismatic move in our congregation. Today, that church building is a pizza parlor, however, those who embraced the Spirit continue to have a great impact for Christ.

An Unexpected Offer

Garth's life revolved around providing for the family.

Even though he came from a background which didn't encourage education, he realized that with the GI bill, he could go to school and better himself.

It was back to double duty. He started college and took a job at a can company as a night watchman. He remained a full time student until he received his degree—and was given a job in the accounting department of the same company. It was his major.

The firm offered to transfer him to the Chicago area, which would mean a significant career advancement.

Garth thought getting me to move was going to be a problem, so to soften the blow he said, "If you agree to the offer, I'll start going to church with you and the girls."

Evidently, he didn't know I would have done anything to get out of the area where we lived—which was so depressing.

You can imagine the joy this brought me. I had spent countless hours in prayer for Garth and now, almost overnight, he was promising to attend church with me and our daughters.

It's often like this with God. We must remain faithful and obedient even when it seems nothing is happening. Why? Because unknown to us, He is working behind the scenes, answering our prayers in glorious ways.

"THIS GUY IS SMART!"

When we arrived in Chicago, Garth picked up a newspaper and read about a new minister who had just relocated to the area. His name was Dr. Clarence Fast.

What impressed my husband was the long list of degrees the clergyman held. He showed me the pastor's picture and said, "This is where we are going to church. This guy is smart—not like your crazy friends!"

Little did Garth know that Dr. Fast not only had his degrees, but also taught and preached the baptism in the Holy Spirit and had a strong altar ministry—the whole nine yards!

It was in this church my husband ultimately made a firm decision to restore his life in Christ. He couldn't prove Dr. Fast wrong, nor me.

The minister was brilliant—a great teacher and mentor for me personally. I volunteered as his secretary and we were blessed by his life.

It was also what Garth needed. Dr. Fast had enough letters after his name to impress him as well as a powerful ministry in the Word and the Spirit. Under his leadership, Garth grew in faith and was baptized in water, along with our daughter Julie.

Garth had some real encounters with God and began to learn about the ministry of the Spirit. In that church a prophetic word was given to him that concerned a vision for his future.

AN ULTIMATUM!

The Lord made wonderful changes in our home because of this anointed minister. I believe it is important for people to attend church regularly, and we were now together as a family, being fed by the Word.

Plus, we were relating to other believers in the body of Christ.

Garth became motivated to study the Bible— especially regarding the baptism of the Holy Spirit (a subject on which he still vehemently disagreed with me).

In one service, Garth's nicotine habit got the best of him and he told the Lord, "Either you take this desire away from me or I'm not going any further with You."

Not only did the Lord deliver him of his cigarette

addiction, he was gloriously filled with the baptism of the Holy Spirit!

What a total transformation had come to our home.

ANOTHER MOVE?

At the same time, Garth was progressing in his career and also academically, earning his Master of Business Administration degree.

Then came another promotion with the company and I was asked, "Honey, are you ready to move to Cleveland?"

Perhaps it was because I had been uprooted so often in life, or because I knew another spiritual adventure was just around the corner, it didn't faze me. I said, "Sure. Let's go!"

CHAPTER 3

A DIVINE ASSIGNMENT

God works in wondrous ways!

When we arrived in Cleveland I thought, "Oh, there's never going to be a church like the others I've known!"

We visited several congregations, but our souls were hungry for fellowship with people who knew the reality of the presence of the Holy Spirit in their lives. I read the passage in the Bible where God declared, *"I will pour water on the thirsty land, and streams on the dry ground"* (Isaiah 44:3), and asked God to fulfill that in my heart.

It wasn't long until the Lord led us to the *Christian Centre* in Cleveland. It was a Foursquare church—the International Church of the Foursquare Gospel, which is theologically the same as the Assemblies of God, Open Bible and other Pentecostal denominations.

The church was a regional ministry under the

leadership of pastors Bob and Beverly Hils.

This gifted couple were powerful leaders in the Charismatic move in their denomination. Pastor Bob ranks among the finest Bible teachers I've ever had the privilege of sitting under—and I've heard practically all of them, either on tape or in person. His vivacious wife, Pastor Beverley, had a dynamic ministry in the Spirit.

PREPARATION TIME

Beverly founded an organization called *Radiant Life* in Cleveland—similar to *Women's Aglow Fellowship*. I was honored when she asked me to serve on the board.

We had monthly luncheon meetings and brought in speakers and ministers from all over the country. Those were the days when large numbers attended such meetings. They don't so much any more because powerful ministers are available in their living rooms via Christian television.

Evidently, the Lord was preparing me for a challenge that both Garth and I would soon encounter.

A WORD FROM ABOVE

Suddenly, there was another move on the horizon. The company gave Garth a promotion and asked us to relocate to Cincinnati—in the southern part of Ohio.

From the moment we arrived, I was once again active in ministry. In addition to participating in our church life, I taught neighborhood Bible studies and became active in the *Women's Aglow* fellowship, eventually becoming president of the Cincinnati Chapter and then serving on the Area Board.

Garth and I both taught "Life in the Spirit" seminars. I also produced flyers for the Full Gospel Business Men's Fellowship International, and led praise and worship at our local chapter meetings (even though it was a MEN'S fellowship)!

Beverly Hils was still in Cleveland, however, we worked closely together to share the costs of bringing Spirit-filled leaders into the area. We arranged speaking engagements, conferences and retreats throughout the region—including Pittsburgh, Columbus, Louisville and Lexington.

"I FEEL GOD IS SPEAKING"

During Thanksgiving 1976, Garth and I were attending a regional convention for the Full Gospel Business Men's Fellowship International. It was a huge conference in Cincinnati for the Tri-State Area of Ohio, Indiana and Kentucky.

In one of the meetings, while Kenneth Hagin was speaking, Garth leaned over to me and whispered, "Let's go up to the room, I feel like we should."

It was at that hotel he first shared with me, "I feel

God is speaking to my heart concerning a new ministry He wants us to lead."

We didn't know what, where or how—we just knew the Lord was at work.

"Why Not Us?"

Christian television was in its infancy. In Chicago and Cleveland, during the early 1970s, we had enjoyed wonderful new programs including *The 700 Club* with Pat Robertson and the *PTL* Club. Even earlier, we were grateful our girls had been blessed by children's shows such as *Davey and Goliath,* and *JOT*, a Christian cartoon series carried by even some of the secular stations.

However, when we moved to Cincinnati, we were disappointed we couldn't receive any of these programs.

Garth felt called of God to do something about the situation—and his vision for Christian television was ignited. We were both novices regarding television, but as Garth told me, "Nobody else is doing it. Why not us?"

This wasn't just a casual idea or a concept, it became a burning passion for both of us. We prayed, believed and claimed the airways for the Lord!

"Forget It!"

Putting our faith into action, on May 20, 1977, a corporation was formed called CCC—Cincinnati

Christian Communications. The subtitle was *Tri-State Christian TV* because the signal was designed to serve the tri-state region of southern Ohio, southeastern Indiana and northern Kentucky.

Then began the tedious process of applying to the Federal Communications Commission for a license. When Garth first called the FCC, the man on the line openly laughed and said, "Forget it, there's nothing available in that area."

This is not what the Lord had told us, so we ignored his advice.

THE PERFECT CORNFIELD!

We found an engineer who sat at his computer for three days trying to figure out where you could place a tower that would serve our target counties. At the time, the FCC gave allotments for a broadcast license to regions depending on the population.

That engineer calculated if you place a tower at a certain point and build a 1000 foot "stick" (as they call it in the industry) and provide one million watts of power, it would cover the Dayton—Cincinnati—Richmond, Indiana area, plus parts of northern Kentucky. Since a station was allotted to Richmond, the tower had to be within a certain proximity to provide a city-grade signal there.

The brilliant engineer even pinpointed the cornfield

where the tower should be built. The Lord wonderfully provided the funds so we could put an option on the land. However, because of a mistake, the realtor let the option drop and it was sold to someone else. We were devastated—because the tower *had* to be built on that exact spot, not anywhere else.

After some desperate praying, the other buyer miraculously changed his mind, and we finally were able to purchase the land.

A TEST OF FAITH

Now what we had to do was submit an application to the Federal Communications Commission (FCC) for a television broadcast license. To say it was a challenge is an understatement! Governmental papers and forms are composed of complicated legalese and are measured in pounds rather than pages!

It was necessary to document in quadruplicate we were people worthy of receiving such a public trust, that we were prepared to operate it according to all regulations, and could afford to do so.

We fulfilled all those obligations and continued working to have everything ready for the day we would receive the all-important "Construction Permit." Think of the excited anticipation a young woman feels awaiting her wedding day—a jillion times over!

One year went by, then two—still no word. In those days you didn't ask anyone at the overworked FCC how it was coming along, for fear they would stick your application at the bottom of the pile again, just out of aggravation for being bothered!

The process was a test of faith beyond anything we had expected.

In the meantime, Garth's career as a corporate executive was flourishing and he was traveling internationally. Every spare moment was given to fulfilling the vision for Christian television, but under Garth's direction, much of the work regarding the fledgling ministry fell on my shoulders.

The Lord gave our family perfect timing for the beginning of the ministry. Our oldest daughter, Vicki, graduated from high school that year and was off to Oral Roberts University in Tulsa, Oklahoma. Her life went in another direction in service to God, of which we are very proud. (Perhaps I can tell those details in another book). Our other daughter, Julie, was twelve years old at the time and involved with us in every step—as she is today.

A Unique Team

From the moment we announced our plans, we tried to involve every person we knew. We needed prayer partners, financial supporters and volunteers to spread the word.

We leaned heavily on our association with those in the Charismatic movement. I was still president of

Cincinnati Women's Aglow and Garth was on the board of FGBMFI. Each of these organizations represented a large network of people.

I still marvel at how the Lord brought the team of board members and key supporters together. Each had unique abilities we needed for the task ahead.

Bob Stein and his wife, Ann, lived across the street from us and I don't know how we could have ever started without their encouragement. Then came Carl and Jean Brady—he was a retired naval engineer and she had been a registered nurse. God placed it in their hearts to give themselves to us in the cause of bringing Christian television to the area.

Jim and Kathy Whittington also caught the vision. He was a chemical engineer who worked with Garth.

Our treasurer was a banker named Chuck Payne. We had teamed with him and his wife, Myra, in "Life in the Spirit" seminars. I'll never forget the day he came flying into our house with the first contribution we received at our Post Office box. It was a check for $10 and we were jubilant—praising the Lord!

Brian and Dolly Perkins were a special couple who lived in the presence of God and provided a quiet stability to the ministry.

Sherman Waddle was an insurance representative. He and his wife, Irene, helped in any way possible.

There were so many wonderful people and countless volunteers who joined us—such as FGBMFI president,

Everett Webb, Jim and Esther Beare, Erv and Linda Wolber—I wish I could name them all.

Many of us took turns holding pot luck suppers at each others' homes. (We called them "pot bless.") After food and fellowship, I would lead in praise and worship with my guitar and then we would have a prayer meeting.

Our board of advisors included pastors from the region who believed in our vision. Their spiritual wisdom and counsel was invaluable. Pastor Clyde Miller of First Christian Assembly in Cincinnati was especially encouraging and supportive to us.

SPREADING THE WORD

To learn a little more of what we were getting ourselves into, we drove to CBN in Virginia Beach, and to PTL in Charlotte. Both ministries welcomed us and gave us some of their video tapes of their programming.

We began a newsletter to spread the idea and responded to every invitation to tell congregations about the vision.

Since we had previous experience planning Christian events, we brought in recognized speakers and singers to attract an audience—at breakfasts, luncheons and dinners. Then we'd tell the people what the Lord had placed in our hearts.

When we announced, "We want to build a Christian TV station," the usual response was, "A what?" No one had the foggiest notion of what we were talking about—it was a totally new concept in that region.

A LIVE DEMONSTRATION

To give people a visual picture of what the programming would include, we bought a VCR recorder that played the 3/4-inch tapes, a monitor, three televison cameras and a switcher. They were the bulkiest pieces of equipment I'd ever seen.

We kept them in our basement, but two or three times a week, a board member who owned a van would come by and help us move it all to a church for a live demonstration.

In the services, I would use my guitar and lead the congregation in a time of praise and worship, I really wasn't a singer, nor a great musician, but the Lord somehow graciously used me in those meetings.

Next, Garth would speak, explaining who we were and what we wanted to do. Then we would turn on the monitor and say, "This is what Christian TV looks like. We want to build a station here which will bring you uplifting programming 24 hours a day—if you will help us and support the ministry."

We repeated this literally hundreds of times, day and night. It was very hard work, especially for Garth, who still functioned as a high-powered executive in the corporate world, and at the same time, pioneered a new ministry. But we felt in the center of God's will, and they were joyous days. As I carried out his directions, I felt as happy as a dog chasing a stick!

Once a week volunteers came to our home to pray and work on newsletters and mailings. We had an old Script-o-Matic addressing machine that was a prelude to a computer—an absolute nightmare!

After the first year, we were able to move the operation out of our home. A friend had a large, elegant office suite for his business and there was one portion of it with three small rooms he didn't use. We rented the space and he let us use his copy machine and restroom. We operated out of that little windowless office for five years.

"NOBODY CARES!"

The peaks and valleys during these days were too numerous to count. I can still recall the night Garth was laying prostrate in the middle of the floor, weeping and crying out to God. At one point he lifted his head and cried, "Nobody cares! Nobody cares!"

They did, but it was difficult to perceive at the time.

In God's providence, He sent some of His choice servants to encourage us—people like Russ Bixler and Lester Sumrall. With great wisdom, Sumrall told us, "If God has called you to this ministry, don't let anybody talk you out of it. But if He has not called you, don't let anybody talk you into it!"

He was right. Satan is the prince of the power of the air, and invading his territory involves intense spiritual warfare.

When viewers watch Garth on television today, it is difficult for them to believe he never felt called to run the station—only to obtain the license and establish the ministry. He had no intention of leaving his job in the corporate world.

WKOI—CHANNEL 43

What a day of rejoicing it was when, in 1982, the FCC granted the license and construction permit for Channel 43 in Richmond, Indiana.

Part of the application for the license was selecting the call letters for the station. Being east of the Mississippi River, they had to begin with a "W." We requested WKOI.

We decided on those letters because they would stand for "**W**inning **K**entucky, **O**hio and **I**ndiana." They were also the first three letters of the word *koinonia*—the Greek word for the rich and loving fellowship within the body of Christ. We knew more and more people would come to know that fellowship through the ministry of Christian television.

We even found a spiritual symbolism in the channel number 43 since 4+3 = 7, God's number of perfection.

GIVE IT AWAY?

Calls of congratulations were flowing in from everywhere—including people we didn't even know. They said, "We've been praying for you."

After five years of constant toil, the vision was close to reality. I asked Garth, "Now what do we do?"

"Remember," he replied, "the Lord never told me to operate this station, only to get it started. We are going to give it away to a Christian organization and let them run it. Our work is finished!"

Garth had been impressed with the ministry of the Trinity Broadcasting Network (TBN) in California, even though we had never met the founders, Paul and Jan Crouch. "I think we should let them operate the station," he told me. They were developing many creative programs and were building television facilities.

The phone call to TBN was one we will never forget. Garth reached Crouch's secretary who politely told him, "Mr. Crouch is not available, but may I ask what this is in regards to?"

Garth told the secretary, "I want to give him a television station."

Two seconds later, Paul Crouch was on the phone, saying, "Hello there, Garth."

MISSION ACCOMPLISHED

We had completed the task. Garth continued traveling around the world in his corporate work. Julie graduated from high school and followed her sister to ORU in Tulsa. With a closed office and an empty house, I went back to school at the University of Cincinnati.

Christian television was beaming its message to our area 24 hours a day and touching countless lives.

We thought this was the end of the story. Little did we know it was only the beginning!

CHAPTER 4

"I NEED YOUR HELP!"

T he television facility in Richmond was the fifth station of the Trinity Broadcasting Network. Since five is the biblical number of grace, we were delighted to play a part in its inception.

In the process of TBN taking on the station, Paul Crouch asked Garth to fly out to California during one of their fund raising events called a "Praise-A-Thon."

Crouch presented the opportunity to the network viewers, saying, "If you want TBN to have this station, you need to call in during the next hour and let us know."

Within 60 minutes more than $250,000 was raised. Garth had never seen anything like it!

The grand opening and dedication was more like a revival meeting than a ribbon cutting, with music by Laverne and Edith Tripp and their family. Steve Brock, one of the nation's finest voices, was also there. At the time he was pastoring a successful church in nearby Hamilton, Ohio.

Actually, the first time Steve appeared on Christian television was when we were starting out and had some studio equipment at our home. We taped several programs in our living room to be aired on cable, and Steve was one of the musical guests. I can still see him standing against those royal blue curtains!

"What's the Difficulty?"

After the dedication of TBN's new station, we rejoiced at the lives being touched for the Gospel.

Our routine returned to normal—Garth was immersed in his corporate work and I was involved in additional college studies and helping with women's ministries in the Cincinnati region.

About two years later, Garth received a call from Paul Crouch, saying, "We are facing a problem with FCC rules and regulations and I believe you are the person to assist in solving the dilemma. I need your help."

"What's the difficulty?" Garth inquired.

At this time, the Federal Communications Commission permitted an organization or individual to own only a limited number of broadcast stations. TBN already had their allotted number—yet new opportunities in larger markets were opening up as they moved forward.

Since they were already at the cap, Paul asked Garth, "Would you be interested in purchasing stations and affiliating with TBN, in the same way local stations affiliate with national networks?"

THE PROPOSAL

One was Marion, Illinois, and the other in Saginaw, Michigan. The Marion station was already on the air with a secular programing schedule which was now airing TBN's *Praise the Lord* program in prime time. "You could take it over and make it an all-Christian format," he suggested. "I don't want to see these stations lost to the Kingdom."

In addition, a license and construction permit were for sale for a station in Saginaw.

From his earlier dealings, Crouch knew my husband was a man of integrity who was not seeking anything of his own. He also knew Garth was an astute, gifted businessman.

Because Trinity Broadcasting Network could not own those stations, Paul proposed an "affiliation agreement." This meant we would develop our own identity—and not be a TBN clone. They could not control us, yet would pay us to air some of their programs. It sounded like a win-win situation.

"WE NEED TO PRAY!"

Garth couldn't give Paul Crouch an instant answer. After all, this was a monumental, turning-point decision, one which would mean a total upheaval of our lives—including losing the security of the corporate lifestyle. Such a commitment would require Garth to leave his career, move to another city and dive head-long, full-time into Christian television.

"Honey, we need to pray," he told me. "This means all your plans will have to change too, because I won't even consider it unless you are with me all the way."

Day after day, we prayed earnestly for God's direction and at every turn the Lord was saying, "Yes. I want you to help build My Kingdom."

It was a giant leap of faith, but Garth picked up the phone and told Paul Crouch, "We'll do it!"

NEW PIONEERS

During the first months, after cutting our anchors loose and sailing into this new adventure, we set up an office in Cincinnati—driving six hours in a van to Marion, and the same to Saginaw.

Establishing the stations was an enormous task, yet there was great joy on the journey. Those who have been pioneers in ministry have experienced the same thing.

Like a farmer, you find supernatural strength to clear

a field, dig out the rocks and plant the first crops. It's almost as exciting as the harvest!

Today, I look back and think, "How in the world did we do that?"

I can still remember the first day the Saginaw station was about to go on the air. After the long drive, we stopped at a gas station to freshen up—and I washed my hair in the bathroom sink. As you know, gas station rest rooms are not the cleanest places in the world, but it met the need at the moment. We needed to look our best, even for the few viewers who would watch the first live broadcast!

JUST ONE SHOW?

One stifling-hot summer morning we were at a motel in Marion—commuting from Cincinnati—getting ready to drive to the station for a day of work. Garth turned to me and said, "Tina, I want you to tape a program today. What do you want to call it?"

I had made some brief appearances with Garth on television, but now he was asking me to host my own program.

As my mind raced, trying to think of what I would teach, and what would be an appropriate title, I blurted out, "Radiant Life."

I thought to myself, "I'll do this one time, using Beverly Hil's title—and it will never be used again.

Besides, she is ten hours away in Cleveland, and will never know."

For many years I had been comfortable speaking before "live" audiences—it was easy since the people would literally *draw* the best out me. But this was totally different.

I figured I would just tape one program and Garth would see it wasn't my specialty. He would surely get the notion out of his system.

In the studio, waiting for the red light to come on for my first show, I stood there quaking in my shoes. My eyes darted all around as I tried to communicate with a stone-cold technological thing called a camera!

Several hundred *Radiant Life* programs later, it was a favorite with viewers, as with my co-hosts, Jan Bishop and later Nancy Starkweather, I interviewed women from all walks of Christian life at each of our stations.

I did, however, write Beverly, asking for her permission to use her title. She graciously agreed.

MOVING TO MARION

It wasn't long until we realized it would be impossible to operate both television stations from a distance. We needed to set up a permanent base of operation and move to one of the two cities.

Since southern Illinois was closer to Tulsa, we decided to move there, rather than Saginaw—because after graduating from ORU, our daughter, Vicki, had married and remained in Tulsa, as had our daughter, Julie.

Our start into full-time Christian television wasn't a giant leap forward, rather it was a series of small steps.

The decisions being made were out of necessity. For example, neither Garth or myself had any desire to be on camera, yet in order to raise the funds to continue, we had to establish a personal relationship with the viewers.

I shudder to think what today's savvy viewers would think of our early broadcasts. The facility in Marion was an old radio station which had been converted for TV. A tiny studio was situated in the basement.

Our sets were created from materials we bought at dime stores and garage sales. Both the sets and the stations' offices were decorated with items brought from our home (and many still are).

I remember the garden we designed for one of our early programs. Cut out pieces of paper served as "stepping stones" winding through the plastic plants on fake grass. Not exactly network quality, but we did the best with what we had!

Behind the scenes, however, Garth was making sound business decisions and keeping the ship on a steady course. He not only had a heavy anointing, but also stability and structure.

During this period, there were a number of ministers who attempted to launch Christian television stations. They were godly men, yet most failed because they did not have the business acumen to handle the intense work involved.

NEW PROGRAMS

Early in the ministry we launched the *TCT Today* program. It was a way to communicate directly with our viewers and let them know what was happening in the network, and why. We also started an interview/music format program for local personalities and ministers to have a place in the schedule, as well as to take advantage of any visiting preachers, teachers, evangelists and musicians who were in town and would share with our viewers.

In the beginning the program was called *Tri-State Alive* and evolved through the years to become the present *TCT Alive.*

We also began the *Public Report* program to address issues of our local community.

Later, we expanded the Marion flagship station with a new "Studio B." Finally, we had the space necessary to produce top-notch programs.

For the first few years we constantly worked day and night. There was never time for a vacation, yet we loved it! I would often tell myself, "This is what I was made to do"—whether it was cleaning the toilets, decorating sets, doing administrative or clerical work, or hosting programs. It was all for the Kingdom.

Sure, we made mistakes, but we did our best and God blessed our efforts.

STANDING BY OUR SIDE

Many ministers of the gospel helped our fledgling ministry in countless ways. So many beloved faces flash through my mind. Some were in the beginning, some were at various points along the way, and some have stayed with us through the years. Each one has been a gracious gift of God serving in a specific way, whatever the time.

I'd love to honor each and every one by giving their names. But I know, regardless of the best intentions, the passage of time and the limitations of human memory would combine to present a less than complete list.

Rather than risk causing even one to feel left out, I'll just say this: It's wonderful to know the accounts are perfectly recorded in heaven. God knows their names and the value of their differing contributions to the ministry. He is more than able to reward for it all, both in personal and professional lives. The same is true for all who have given financially for full time Christian television.

STEP BY STEP

We serve a God who understands the value of small

beginnings. If we take care of the little things, He will do the rest.

It's inspiring to have lofty dreams, but the path to success in the Kingdom is to allow the Lord to show you His direction and quietly be obedient day after day, step by step.

As we will discuss later in this book, I have been careful to recognize the vision God has given to my husband. I honor and appreciate the fact he has been chosen by the Lord to lead this ministry. It is in this context I offer him my best counsel and advice. Sometimes he says, "That's good," and at other times he responds, "Well, let me think about that."

Fortunately, I am married to a man who isn't easily swayed by people. Instead, he hears from God and has enough courage to move forward regardless of what others think.

Has he made mistakes during the growth of TCT? Of course, and since we are in a public ministry, any miscues are magnified. Yet, by staying true to his calling, keeping his heart pure and never losing hope, the errors become learning lessons on the road to fulfilling God's vision.

The ministry was in it's infancy, but it was about to take wings!

CHAPTER 5

THE BEST SEAT

The frequent travel between Marion and Saginaw was not only taking a toll on our van, but on our physical bodies. By the time we reached each station we were exhausted—yet people expected us to arrive with recharged batteries.

One evening, after Garth had given his personal testimony at a Full Gospel Business Men's Fellowship meeting, a man named Bob Allen took my husband aside and asked to speak with him.

"I'm an electrical contractor from Benton, Illinois, but I have been an aviator for many years," he said. "I believe what you need is an airplane to commute between your stations and I'd like to give you one."

This was beyond our imagination, yet something we desperately needed. When he presented us with a used twin-engine Cessna 310, we were thrilled beyond words.

Instead of making a big splash out of the donation to the ministry, Garth went to work on obtaining his pilot's license. This wasn't a toy, rather a timely gift from God for the purpose of spreading the Gospel efficiently.

"I Don't Have Time!"

Normally, it takes about one year to be licenced, but Garth was a certified pilot in three months!

He then urged me to obtain my license, yet since I was so busy at the station, I made the excuse, "I don't have time!"

Those words weren't in Garth's vocabulary so one day he made an appointment with a flight instructor and said, "Honey, you're going to be there."

I soon learned why he insisted I take the lessons—because he needed me as his co-pilot. While earning my license, I learned the importance of "life in the right seat"—not just in the air, but in every aspect of our relationship. After all, I wouldn't be doing any of the things I'm responsible for if it were not for the man to whom I am married.

Capable, But Not in Charge

Many planes require a two-man crew. The one in the left seat is called the PIC—pilot in command. He is responsible for everything that happens on the flight, from beginning to end. However, the person in the right seat has to be as fully equipped, knowledgeable and as capable as the one in the left seat. For example, he has to be able to handle the airplane if the PIC loses consciousness—as has happened in aviation.

In the middle of a flight, he or she must be fully competent to respond to any emergency. The individual must be trained and, like the pilot, take periodic refresher courses. The right-seat pilot is *capable*, but not in charge.

This is exactly how God designed marriage to work. Even in organizations, there are many people who are qualified to handle things for awhile, yet only one person can be totally in control.

FACING THE STORMS

In flight, the pilot in charge may turn over temporary control while he tends to some other matter, however, this does not mean the second-in-command makes the important decisions concerning the flight.

This mirrors my relationship with Garth. He makes the choices, while I help whenever I can—and am totally capable of handling things in an emergency.

When we've tried using other trained pilots it has never worked out because Garth has yet to find a pilot he believes is as proficient as himself. That is not ego talking, just fact—he is an excellent pilot.

Yes, there have been some scary situations. This is true for anyone who flies a great deal—or who drives a car thousands of miles.

There's a saying that "flying is hours and hours of boredom punctuated by moments of terror."

Once, when Garth first began flying, we found ourselves in some inclement weather that was really atrocious. I'm still not sure whether it was the Lord or my husband's skill which pulled us through the mess, but they are a great team!

There have been times when we suddenly found ourselves wrapped in what pilots call "soup." You can hardly see past the propellers and you are totally dependent on your instruments—and your ability to read them correctly.

MY TURN!

Once, our roles were reversed and Garth was seated on the right side. This was just after his heart bypass surgery.

After such a procedure it's a complicated process for a pilot to regain his medical approval and be reinstated. The FAA is merciless in their demands—and there are many hoops to jump through.

During this time, when I was legal to fly (but not Garth), we flew into some really bad weather. The plane was hopping all over the sky and our heads were bouncing off the ceiling!

I still remember Garth telling me from the right seat,

"Don't worry. It's going to be all right."

The pressure was intense and I realized I was the person legally responsible at that precise moment. I don't know who was more relieved when the weather cleared, Garth or myself!

TIME FOR A CHECK-UP

Air safety requires that every two years you have a flight review—a complete re-examination of your skills and knowledge.

I often think, "Wouldn't it be wonderful if every Christian were required to have a bi-annual spiritual checkup?" Think what would happen if we stood before God to answer questions concerning our knowledge of the Word and our competence to represent the Father.

As I've mentioned, the FAA also insists on excellent health and the ability to pass certain medical exams. Nothing is to interfere with your ability to fly the plane safely.

For example, alcohol is absolutely forbidden. There's a saying among pilots: "Eight hours from bottle to throttle." However, since many professional pilots are always "on call," they *never* touch alcohol.

This should be a lesson for all believers since the Lord desires our minds to be clear and focused, ready to follow His commands.

A MARVELOUS TOOL

On rare occasions we have been criticized by jealous people for owning a plane, but they soon learn this gift from God has been a marvelous tool for the ministry. It is not used for pleasure-flying, rather to transport us from station to station to conduct the business at hand.

To Garth and me, the plane is an instrument of TCT— no different than a camera or computer. We utilize it honestly in the Lord's work, not for any personal satisfaction.

DON'T REBEL AGAINST LEADERSHIP

It is important for the most qualified person to be in the pilot's chair.

This is the way it is with Garth and me, both in aviation and in ministry. He is light years ahead in his capabilities and has thousands of hours of flight time—and that's what is most important in the air.

Often, when others think they can perform at the same level as the leader, conflicts arise in both personal relationships and in the Lord's work

In the Old Testament there is a story of Korah who gathered 250 children of Israel together in a rebellion against Moses and Aaron, saying, *"You have gone far enough, for all the congregation are holy, every one of them, and the Lord is in their midst; so why do you exalt yourselves above the assembly of the Lord?"* (Numbers 16:3).

What was God's response to those who rose up against His chosen leaders? The earth opened up and the followers of Korah fell into the pit and were destroyed (v.32).

Read what happened to Moses' sister, Miriam, when she spoke against her brother because of the Ethiopian woman he had married. She questioned, *"Has the Lord indeed spoken only through Moses?"* (Numbers 12:2).

She paid a price for resenting Moses' decision-making and turned *"leprous, as white as snow"* (v.10).

This is what happens when people reject the order God establishes for His designated leader.

A LINE OF AUTHORITY

Today, those in ministry need to guard their thoughts and attitudes, realizing the Lord places people into positions of authority, in government and in life. There must be a structure, and somebody must be in charge.

In many ways, God is saying, "You need to function within My order. Don't resist or make it more difficult for the person in charge—his job is hard enough."

According to scripture, the headship of a home rests with the husband and father; he has the ultimate responsibility for what is taking place and answers to

God. As a result, the man carries a weight those under him cannot fully comprehend.

No Agenda

The reason I am so comfortable in the right seat is because I know it is God's pattern for my life. As Paul the Apostle says, *"I have learned to be content in whatever circumstances I am"* (Philippians 4:11).

Even if I *could* do things differently, I wouldn't want to. Why? Because I realize it is the Lord who has placed me next to my husband—and that he is to be in charge.

Sure, I give input into many situations, but I don't have an agenda to push. Rather, I yield to the decisions of the appointed leader—my husband.

Even if a wife disagrees with the direction her spouse is taking, it's better to pray for the situation than draw battle lines and turn the home into a war zone. Never forget the Lord can change the heart of a king in the direction He desires it to turn (Proverbs 21:1).

As wives, we must be willing to trust God for answers—not to make shipwrecks of our lives by insisting we have things our own way.

The Right Combination

It is virtually impossible for two equally strong

leaders to live together peaceably—they will devour one another! The reason opposites attract is because one person supplies what may be lacking in the other.

Garth and I have discussed this matter and concluded I was drawn to him because of his strength of character, and he was attracted to me because he saw the tenderness and softness he lacked.

By putting the right combination together, we have a marriage which works beautifully—with each of us understanding and performing our role. There is a healthy balance.

In the Bible, Pricilla and Aquilla are an example of a man and wife working together in ministry (Acts 18).

Even today, some look at high-profile couples in God's work and say, "I want to be like them." However, they don't have a clue regarding the price that has been paid for the relationship. There have been years spent in development of character, reshaping it into an obedience and willingness to serve the Lord.

The healing evangelist, Kathryn Kuhlman once said, "No one will ever know what this ministry cost me."

If you are going to serve God fully—and publicly—the price will be steep.

OTHERS, NOT OURSELVES

A single person should never seek a mate just for the purpose of being married. He or she needs to ask themselves, "What do I have to contribute and offer that would be desirable and helpful?"—not "What is that person going to give me?"

In scripture, the path to fulfilment requires being more concerned about others than ourselves. Remember, the Son of God was willing to sacrifice His life for *our* benefit, even when we did not understand or appreciate what He gave.

Our happiness will only come when we follow in the Lord's footsteps. Jesus had much to say concerning masters, slaves, employers, employees and our personal relationships, but the bottom line is this: *"In everything...treat people the same way you want them to treat you...in honour preferring one another"* (Matthew 7:12; Romans 12:10 KJV).

A TIME TO KEEP SILENT

When things aren't going your way, there is no advantage to stomping off in a huff, demanding your own way, or worse, angrily defending yourself with accusations. The Bible says, *"Christ suffered for you, leaving you an example, that you should follow in his steps....When they hurled their insults at him, he did not retaliate; when he suffered, he made no threats. Instead, he entrusted himself to him who judges justly"* (1 Peter 2:21,23).

There's a time to speak and a time to remain silent.

When you commit yourself to the Lord, it's much better to close you lips and allow Him to handle the matter. God can fight our battles much more efficiently than we ever can.

A MUZZLE?

When discussing the role of women, many refer to the "no no" scriptures in the New Testament where women are told to keep silent in church. If you study those passages and understand what they mean historically, culturally and contextually, it doesn't mean a muzzle is to be placed on women as if they are inferior creatures. No. In the Hebrew culture women were respected and what they said was listened to.

The Bible is filled with examples of women with significant ministries who were highly esteemed:

- Dorcas (also known as Tabitha) served the Lord in the early church and was well respected for her service to others (Acts 9:36-42).
- Paul gives Eunice and Lois credit for sharing their faith with Timothy (1 Timothy 1:5).
- The four daughters of Philip were prophetesses (Acts 21:9).

"A Gentle and Quiet Spirit"

There has been much discussion of the fact woman are to be adorned with *"the imperishable quality of a gentle and quiet spirit, which is precious in the sight of God"* (1 Peter 3:4).

Does this mean the woman has no rights or privileges and is not deserving of any respect? Is she a doormat who never opens her mouth about anything?

Today, in some Middle Eastern societies, women are cloaked and have no more than the privileges of a pet! As a result, entire societies are hindered in development because they are only using half of their population.

This is not God's pattern.

The Attitude Inside

In an oft-quoted passage, Paul tells young Timothy, *"I want the men in every place to pray, lifting up holy hands, without wrath and dissension. Likewise, I want women to adorn themselves with proper clothing, modestly and discreetly, not with braided hair and gold or pearls or costly garments, but rather by means of good works, as is proper for women making a claim to godliness"* (1 Timothy 2:8-10).

These words have been often misapplied and become a bondage—which is not the Father's intent.

At one time, God's people melted their valuable jewelry and turned it into an idolatrous golden calf. Now He is looking for moderation in women—not that she looks like a dowdy housewife, but that she is decent, well dressed, with good taste and propriety.

This is not about covering your neck and arms, or measuring the length of your skirt; it concerns the attitude of your heart.

What scripture teaches is ladylike behavior that people will respect—a life that is decent and in order.

CHOOSING QUIETNESS

Next we read, *"A woman must quietly receive instruction with entire submissiveness. But I do not allow a woman to teach or exercise authority over a man, but to remain quiet. For it was Adam who was first created, and then Eve. And it was not Adam who was deceived, but the woman being deceived, fell into transgression. But women will be preserved through the bearing of children if they continue in faith and love and sanctity with self-restraint"* (vv.11-16).

By studying the original language you will discover this silence is a *voluntary* sort of muzzling—or *choosing* to remain quiet when you have perfect authority, ability and qualifications to speak to a situation.

The Greek noun for "quiet" used here is *hesuchia,* meaning "a peaceful surrounding."

The same word is used earlier in this chapter when Paul says, *"I urge that entreaties and prayers, petitions and thanksgivings, be made on behalf of all men, for kings and all who are in authority, so that we may lead a tranquil and quiet life in all godliness and dignity"* (1 Timothy 2:1-2).

We are to make entreaties, prayers and petitions for all who are in authority. Why? So we can live in *hesuchia*—*"a tranquil and quiet life in all godliness and dignity."*

A PLACE FOR PEACE

The Lord desires for women to place a guard over their mouth so as not to spew out things indiscriminately. The Greek verb *sigao* is used in scripture, meaning "to keep silent and hold one's peace" (1 Corinthians 14:27-28). It is making the decision not to speak in a given situation, for the greater good of the whole. You might be able to, and even have a right to speak, but you have the wisdom (or good sense) to know when to speak or not.

A female should not be throwing hysterical fits, jabbering about her thoughts or opinions and telling everyone else what to do—especially men!

A woman may actually be wiser and more intelligent than men she comes in contact with, yet if she starts throwing her "smarts" around, she will make enemies and wonder why no one chooses to be near her.

What is needed? The woman must discipline or "sigao" herself so there can be a peaceable ambiance around her.

This is a basic principle of God's Word.

THE RIGHT DECISION

I have been asked, "Tina, would you be sitting in the right seat if you were married to someone else?"

Thank God, He placed me with exactly the right person. The Lord made both of us to be the personalities we are and intends for us to compliment one another.

Working together means someone must be willing to sit in the right seat. It doesn't infer such a person has nothing to bring to the table—or is incapable of flying the plane when necessary. Instead, the individual voluntarily yields to the authority of the pilot in command and to the choices and decisions he makes.

I have learned from experience that the right seat is the *best* seat!

CHAPTER 6

THE POWER OF INFLUENCE

I was once asked, "Tina, if you had to name the greatest power a woman possesses, what would it be?"

To me, there is only one answer: "The power of influence."

While men are the decision makers, women are blessed with an amazing ability to mold and shape the choices he makes. However, danger is involved since there is a fine line between influence and manipulation.

We should never forget what took place in the Garden of Eden. Before Adam was presented with a wife, God gave him this one command: *"From any tree of the garden you may eat freely; but from the tree of the knowledge of good and evil you shall not eat, for in the day that you eat from it you will surely die"* (Genesis 2:16-17).

Then, after Eve was formed from Adam's rib, the serpent came along with his lie, encouraging the woman to eat of the tree, telling her, *"You surely will not die! For God knows that in the day you eat from it your eyes will be opened, and you will be like God, knowing good and evil"* (Genesis 3:4-5).

Not only did Eve bite into the fruit, she *"gave also to her husband, and he ate"* (v.6). Adam sinned because he succumbed to the power of her influence.

"MY LORD"

Let me share with you a story from the Bible about a woman who not only experienced life in the right seat, she had a subtle yet powerful impact on her husband.

The account of Sarah and Abraham is well documented, but it's important to know the level of respect she had for the man who was called "the father of nations." Sarah called her husband, *"my lord"* (Genesis 18:12).

This tells us she considered Abraham to be the head of the household, the one who made the decisions—acknowledging his authority.

If you read the entire story, you learn that Sarah was hardly a dainty wallflower. She was a strong-willed woman capable of holding her own and the influence she wielded over Abraham was substantial.

In her own way, she pushed an idea on her husband until he yielded—and today we are still living with the consequences of her actions.

God had promised Abraham and Sarah a child, but after many years she was still barren. So Sarah concocted a way to fulfill her dream.

Since the couple was wealthy enough to have an assortment of servants, Sarah suggested to Abraham he lie with one of her handmaidens, an Egyptian whose name was Hagar. According to scripture, she told her husband, *"Now behold, the Lord has prevented me from bearing children. Please go in to my maid; perhaps I will obtain children through her"* (Genesis 16:2).

Obviously, Abraham loved his wife so much he agreed to her wishes—even though it was contrary to the original promise the Almighty had made.

An Unwise Decision

The practice of fathering children through servants was widely used in those days—since such women were considered part of the family. In this case, however, it was completely out of God's will. It also speaks powerfully about the problems created through surrogate motherhood.

Sarah persuaded Abraham to sleep with Hagar and later she "gave forth on her knees." This is an expression used in the time which indicates that when a servant gave birth, the mistress of the house would literally be physically present to receive the child from the birth canal and place it on her knees so it would be legally her child —even though it wasn't biologically.

The child born into the household was named Ishmael.

THE WRONG INFLUENCE

Never underestimate the power of generational heritage. Since Hagar was an Egyptian, she was likely influenced by pagan beliefs.

Although the topic of nature vs. nurture is hotly debated, many researchers believe much of our behavior is a result of genetics rather than being shaped by experience and environment.

Even though Ishmael was technically Abraham's son, Bible scholars believe he was raised by Hagar as part of her nomadic society—and she taught him during his formative years.

The real miracle occurred when Abraham was 100 years old and Sarah was 90. God fulfilled His promise and she gave birth to a son—Isaac.

A JEALOUS BROTHER

At the age of three—when he was to be weaned—Abraham threw a big party for Isaac. The celebration was in honor of the milestone reached by his son who was destined to eventually become head of the household.

Young Ishmael stood in the corner, watching this new

kid come along who had all the rights and privileges, while he had nothing. So he mocked and made fun of the event. After all, Ishmael had no respect for the spiritual heritage involved—he had received no prior training.

What happened? Sarah demanded of Abraham, *"Drive out this maid and her son, for the son of this maid shall not be an heir with my son Isaac"* (Genesis 21:10).

The matter distressed Abraham greatly, yet he yielded to Sarah because she raised such a fuss—and he wanted peace in the household.

AN ETERNAL CONFLICT

The series of events may sound cruel by today's standards, yet this was part of life in a desert society and the way people survived.

As Hagar and Ishmael were leaving, *"Abraham rose early in the morning and took bread and a skin of water and gave them to Hagar, putting them on her shoulder, and gave her the boy, and sent her away. And she departed and wandered about in the wilderness of Beersheba"* (v.14).

They would have perished if God had not intervened, sending an angel to show her where there was some water and shade—to assure her that she and the boy would not die of thirst, but the Lord would *"make a great nation of him"* (v.18).

Sarah's behavior was wrong—both in arranging the

birth of Ishmael through Hagar, and later influencing Abraham to evict the two out of the household.

Ishmael eventually married an Egyptian (v.21) and became the father of those we know today as Arabs. This was the genesis of the conflict between Arabs and Jews in the Middle East which continues to this very day.

A WOMAN NAMED ESTHER

Later in the Old Testament, we discover a marvelous example of a woman who used her influence in the midst of a horrible situation. It's the remarkable story of Esther.

King Ahasuerus, ruler of the vast Persian Empire, threw a party at his palace to show off his wealth and power. The event lasted for an incredible 180 days—with special guests from the kingdom invited at different times.

One night, the king wanted to impress his guests with the beauty of his wife, Queen Vashti, and called for her to attend, wearing her crown. However, she was giving her own reception for women and refused to make an appearance before her husband's drunken friends.

This upset the king to such an extent he issued a royal edict declaring, *"...Vashti may no longer come into the presence of King Ahasuerus, and let the king give her royal position to another who is more worthy than she"* (Esther 1:19).

He was using his wife as an object lesson to show his

subjects that *all* wives should be submissive and obey their husbands.

THE BEAUTY CONTEST

To find a new queen, the king called for a national beauty pageant—and the winner would replace Vashti.

In the land there were exiled Jews living among the Persians—including a beautiful young woman named Esther, an orphan raised by her uncle, Mordecai.

He told Esther to enter the contest, but to keep her Jewish heritage a secret. She dutifully obeyed him and was chosen as one of the candidates.

Here was a woman caught up in a situation which was not of her own making—she had no rights of any kind. Manipulated and controlled by everyone around her, what did Esther do? Did she rail against her fate, plotting to change the circumstances?

No. She submitted herself to Hegai, the king's eunuch, who was in charge of the harem.

For the next year, all of those vying for the position stayed at the palace and were given beauty treatments in preparation for the moment they would be presented before the king.

Finally, when King Ahasuerus made his choice, Esther was proclaimed the Queen of Persia.

AN EVIL PLOT

Esther continued to keep in contact with Mordecai by sending emissaries to meet him outside the palace walls. This is how she eventually learned two of the kings ministers, Bigthan and Teresh had plotted to kill Ahasuerus.

When Esther told the king what Mordecai had shared with her, he ordered the two plotters to be killed. Ahaseurus then promoted a man named Haman as his senior officer.

In that position, people of the land were to bow before Haman, but Mordecai refused—knowing that bowing down to another person was forbidden by his Jewish faith.

This so angered Haman he plotted the destruction of not only Mordecai, but of all the Jews living in the kingdom. By consulting astrologers and casting lots, he decided his evil plan of extermination should take place one year later.

In order to obtain the king's approval for his deceptive plan, Haman told Ahaseurus, *"There is a certain people scattered and dispersed among the peoples in all the provinces of your kingdom; their laws are different from those of all other people and they do not observe the king's laws, so it is not in the king's interest to let them remain. If it is pleasing to the king, let it be decreed that they be destroyed, and I will pay ten thousand talents of silver into the hands of those who carry on the king's business, to put into the king's treasuries"* (Esther 3:8-9).

"WHAT CAN I DO?"

As you can imagine, the Jews were greatly distressed and Mordecai sent word to Esther, begging her to plead with the king to spare the lives of her people.

She sent back a message, saying, "What can I do? The king hasn't called for me in a month. If I approach him without being called, I could be executed."

Even though she was the queen, Esther could not randomly walk into the king's inner chamber without his invitation. Mordecai passed the word to her with this challenge: *"And who knows whether you have not attained royalty for such a time as this?"* (Esther 4:14).

Knowing the cost, Esther made the courageous decision to approach the king, telling Mordecai, *"...if I perish, I perish"* (v.16).

CHASTE AND RESPECTFUL BEHAVIOR

After fasting for three days, she bravely stepped into the royal throne room and stood quietly. She understood the protocol she had breached and what would be the terrible result of his displeasure. Suddenly, King

Ahasuerus held out his golden scepter and she reached out to touch it. The king then asked, *"What is troubling you, Queen Esther? And what is your request? Even to half of the kingdom it shall be given to you"* (Esther 5:3).

Such a wild oath was typical Middle Eastern hyperbole, especially for a swaggering potentate committed to his own glorification.

AUTHORITY AND RESPECT

Esther received favor from the king because he knew her character. She had that *"gentle and quiet spirit which is precious in the sight of God"* (1 Peter 3:4). Yet, she had great inner strength. She had exercised authority wisely over her staff and they loved her. Even the men in charge of the harem saw her gracious submission and respected her.

The king didn't see an hysterical female barging in and yelling at him! No. Esther quietly used her influence to fulfill the will of God for her people.

That evening she prepared a banquet for both the king and Haman. Obviously, she knew the old adage, "The way to a man's heart is through his stomach," and she possessed the feminine skill of knowing how to prepare and hostess an elegant event.

When the event concluded, the king couldn't sleep and asked one of his valets to read the chronicle of the events during the 12 years of his reign. God used that time to remind Ahasuerus of Mordecai's good deed five years earlier when he revealed the plot against the king's life.

THE PLOT BACKFIRES

Realizing Mordecai had never been honored, he began making plans to pay tribute to the man. However, that same morning, Haman came by, seeking an early audience with the king for the purpose of asking permission to kill Mordecai publically.

When Haman walked in, King Ahasuerus asked, *"'What is to be done for the man whom the king desires to honor?' And Haman said to himself, 'Whom would the king desire to honor more than me?'"* (Esther 6:6).

Haman, gleefully thinking the king was referring to him, suggested the person be given a special robe, a ride through the city on a noble horse and a prince to announce his arrival (vv.8-9). What a delicious accomplishment! For an ambitious courtier to use the king's apparel and horse was the ultimate in prestige—not to mention the perverse pleasure in being heralded by a royal personage.

What a shock it must have been for Haman when the king ordered, *"...do so for Mordecai the Jew, who is sitting at the king's gate"* (v.10). Devastated, he obeyed the king

THE TABLES ARE TURNED

At Esther's second banquet, with Haman also in attendance, the king asked for her request. It was there, she reveals her own Jewish heritage and says, *"If I have found favor in your sight, O king, and if it pleases the king, let my life be given me as my petition, and my people as my request; for we have been sold, I and my people, to be destroyed, or be killed and to be annihilated. Now if we had only been sold as slaves, men and women, I would have remained silent, for the trouble would not be commensurate with the annoyance to the king"* (Esther 7:3-4).

King Ahasuerus was totally unaware of such a plan, and demanded to know who had plotted such a scheme. Esther pointed to Haman.

The action that followed is worthy of a Hollywood production! The king left the room in stunned fury at the monstrous revelation. Terrified at his sudden exposure, Haman lunged onto Esther's couch to plead for mercy at her feet. Just at that awful moment, the king came back into the room! His rage at seeing Haman accost his queen put the situation beyond recovery. Haman was hanged on the very gallows he had sadistically built for Mordecai.

Because of the influence of Esther, her people were saved. Now, many centuries later, Jews still celebrate the event with the Feast of Purim.

God's name is never mentioned in the book of Esther, yet we can see His mighty hand at work.

"FOR SUCH A TIME AS THIS"

What an example! Esther prayed and asked for wisdom, then she acted discreetly—as the Word asks us to do.

Just as Esther, each of us has *been brought to the Kingdom for such a time as this.* The Bible says God has prepared in advance the good works each of us are supposed to do. As with Esther, if you refuse to do what He has asked you to, He may find someone else to do it, but you will be guilty of disobedience—the reason Saul lost his kingdom. God says obedience is better than sacrifice.

What has God asked you to do? If you are honest with yourself before God, He will speak to your heart and you will know.

"SHUT UP, MIND YOUR OWN BUSINESS, AND GET TO WORK"

In 1 Thessalonians 4:11, we find instructions that are almost humorous. God says we are to "shut up, mind our own business, and get to work." Yes, it really does! Here is how one version expresses it: *"This should be your ambition: to live a quiet life, minding your own business and doing your own work..."*

The Lord wants us to stop complaining, stop looking around at other people, and just do what He has given us to do. When Peter wanted to know what was going to happen to the younger John, Jesus' answer was basically, "Never mind about him. You just do what I tell you to do." Check it out in John 21.

For a believing woman who is married, the charge is clear. Just as Esther did, she behaves in a manner pleasing to God and adapts to her husband's leadership. She submits to his personality and furthers his calling and purpose.

Whatever the situation in which the Lord has placed you, in God's providence, He has prepared you "for such a time as this."

As you seek your Heavenly Father's guidance, He will show you how to use your influence to fulfill His perfect will.

CHAPTER 7

12 STEPS TO A SUCCESSFUL MARRIAGE

Standing before a minister and saying "I do," is the easy part. What will happen when finances become tight, arguments erupt and personality conflicts reach the boiling point?

Some couples shrug their shoulders and say,"Either a marriage works or it doesn't"—and without any effort they are ready to throw in the towel.

A lasting marriage, however, cannot be based just on feelings—they are as unreliable as the stock market! Building a solid, lasting relationship takes a total commitment and diligent work.

Let me share these 12 steps to a successful marriage:

1. Understand the role of submission.

Personally, I've never had a problem with Garth being the head of our household.

In the early years of our marriage, my constant prayer was, "Lord, make me the wife and mother you want me to be—because I don't know how to be either one."

Since, I didn't have training for my role, let alone any example, I asked the Lord to be my guide. Then, when I began to study scripture regarding God's principles for marriage, my place as a wife became clear

Garth and I both have our strengths and weaknesses, yet someone must be in charge—and according to scripture, it is the husband.

The apostle Paul equates the roles of spouses with Christ and the church. He says, *"Wives, be subject to your own husbands, as to the Lord. For the husband is the head of the wife, as Christ also is the head of the church, He Himself being the Savior of the body. But as the church is subject to Christ, so also the wives ought to be to their husbands in everything"* (Ephesians 5:22-24).

The wife who is constantly demanding her rights, advantages and privileges is not only living contrary to God's law, she creates discord in the home.

However just as the woman has a prescribed role in the marriage, so does the husband. He is not to be a dictator or tyrant, but one who treats his wife with esteem and respect. Paul continues, *"Husbands, love your wives, just as Christ also loved the church and gave Himself up for her"* (v.25).

Even more, a man is to love his wife as his own body—for, *"He who loves his own wife loves himself"* (v.28).

True submission is not based on supremacy, rather it is the foundation of love.

2. Be a peacemaker, not a judge.

A yielded wife doesn't mean a woman with no opinions. There are always differences which need to be addressed.

Our marriage is unique since we work together both in the home and in a ministry—with issues to be discussed regarding everything from family finances to corporate decisions.

A man usually sees a goal and goes after it like an arrow flying toward a target. If people want to get on board with his idea, fine. If not, they're out the door!

The woman, however, functions in a much softer fashion—preferring consensus to conflict and team building.

Personally, I've learned not to usurp authority or judge Garth for doing things differently than I would. He has the final decision.

Let me give you another example. A church purchased a new piano and the pastor said, "I think it should go on the left side of the platform."

His wife knew it would throw everything off balance and should be positioned on the right side."

If he disagrees with her opinion, should she talk to other church members and get them to take sides? No. That would cause conflict and perhaps inflict hard feelings which might take months to resolve.

Instead, a considerate wife would chose the path of a peacemaker. The next Sunday morning she would smile and say, "Well, doesn't that piano look good!"

Yes, there will be times when your emotions take over your intellect and you vent your feelings. If that happens, address the problems quickly and resolve them. Remember, the Bible tells us, *"...do not let the sun go down on your anger"* (Ephesians 4:26).

3. Avoid being demanding or controlling.

Over the years I have met women who have come to Christ, yet their husbands refuse to attend church with them or have anything to do with spiritual matters.

Sadly, some wives resort to pressure tactics—including placing a "guilt trip" on their spouse—in an attempt to win them to the Lord. It doesn't work! In fact, it has the opposite effect and can cause a permanent rift in the home.

Here's what the Bible says: *"...a woman who has an unbelieving husband, and he consents to live with her, she must not send her husband away"* (1 Corinthians 7:13).

A demanding or controlling spirit is not of God. In the words of King Solomon, *"It is better to live in a desert land, than with a contentious and vexing woman"* (Proverbs 21:19).

Regardless of the differences of opinion, shower your husband with genuine affection and create an atmosphere of harmony. You will be surprised how the Lord will work on your behalf.

4. Always extend mercy.

Often without intent, spouses wound each other deeply with words or actions. When the stress and pressures of life mount, just one word taken out of context can escalate into a full-blown argument. Many times the problem lies not with the husband or wife, but with outside forces which invade the home.

When the first sign of a disagreement appears, regardless of the cause or who is in the wrong, always be the first to say, "I'm sorry. Please forgive me"

Holding a grudge or harboring an unresolved dispute will only produce seeds of bitterness—which soon sprout thorns. Who is harmed? The one holding onto the anger!

Jesus says, *"For if you forgive others for their transgressions, your heavenly Father will also forgive you"* (Matthew 6:14). Likewise, He declares, *"Blessed are the merciful, for they shall receive mercy"* (Matthew 5:7).

5. Recognize your differences.

For years, I kept a little folder and would write down topics I needed to discuss with Garth. Even though we worked together, there seemed to be no time for personal conversation.

Then, in the evening after a long day at the office, when I would bring up an item from my list, he would often brush me off, preferring to read the paper or watch television and have a little peace and quiet.

Hurt, I wondered, "Is he trying to avoid me, or doesn't he care?" Sometimes I would simmer in resentment, "He talks to everybody but me!"

Finally, I learned that when he's ready to talk, he will.

Women, however, are always ready to have a conversation about what is happening in their world.

Let's face it, men and women are not only different physically, but also emotionally.

It is easy for a woman to love because her emotions vacillate all over the place—we love everything from friends, colors, sunsets, food and shopping. The emotions of love are a natural and integral part of our life and thoughts.

A husband's needs are usually the opposite. He seeks respect and desires to be appreciated for his abilities and strength. Most men thrive on honor and recognition. Connected to that, which many women don't understand, is his natural need for physical fulfillment in the act of marriage.

Because men and women's needs are so different, the Bible gives differing instructions to us. It tells husbands to LOVE their wives, and wives to RESPECT their husbands.

One of the most important conversations any wife and husband can have is to openly discuss those differences. When individual needs are met, the marriage is strengthened.

Remember, as husband and wife you are there to help and encourage one another. When God created the first woman, He said, *"It is not good for the man to be alone; I will make him a helper suitable for him"* (Genesis 2:18).

Are you fulfilling God's desire?

6. *Spend more time listening than speaking.*

Sometimes a husband may have a fear of his wife being with other women. Why? Because he knows how much she loves to gossip—and may reveal an intimate secret.

I have to admit I've been at a few women-only social gatherings where the guests sounded like chickens—"pick, pick, pick, pick, pick!"

The apostle James warns, *"...the tongue is a small part of the body, and yet it boasts of great things. See how great a forest is set aflame by such a small fire! And the tongue is a fire, the very world of iniquity; the tongue is set among our members as that which defiles the entire body, and sets on fire the course of our life, and is set on fire by hell"* (James 3:5-6).

As a wife, make it your objective to spend more time thinking, listening and observing than speaking.

Mary, the mother of Jesus, should be our example. In Bethlehem, when the shepherds came with news of what had been told them concerning this special Child, *"...Mary kept all these things, and pondered them in her heart"* (Luke 2:19 KJV). Even the world recognizes—it is STILL water that runs deep.

7. *Practice true humility.*

Pride is often a ticking time bomb in marriages. A woman can become distracted with the wrong priorities, so consumed by the size of her home, the luxury car she drives and the label on her designer clothes that nothing else matters.

In some cases, *who* she marries is more important than *why.*

Rest assured, God knows our innermost thoughts and there must be no room for arrogance or haughtiness. The Bible admonishes: *"Do nothing from selfishness or empty conceit, but with humility of mind regard one another as more important than yourselves; do not merely look out for your own personal interests, but also for the interests of others"* Philippians 2:3-4).

Never forget, our true possessions have been provided by the Lord—our ability, talent and intellect. He deserves all our praise.

8. *Learn to please your husband.*

We know husbands and wives are to show affection

to each other, but in God's order of things it begins with the woman.

You are instructed to yield yourself and be willing to serve your mate in whatever capacity is needed for his ultimate benefit and welfare. Your purpose is to complete him—providing those things he does not possess.

As you read in an earlier chapter, there were years in our marriage when I was attending church alone. Yet, I was still his wife—and sought to please him in every way possible.

Then, when Garth re-committed his life to the Lord, we began working together and the joy of our relationship blossomed.

9. Demonstrate your love.

I recall a day in Cleveland when our girls were small. We had gone shopping at a mall when suddenly a "lake effect" storm hit and snow was falling fast and furious.

The mall was downhill from where we lived, and in order to make it home we had to drive up a rather steep incline.

Well, cars were all over the place—sliding off the road in ditches and clogging the street.

Concerned, I asked Garth, "What do you think we should do?" I could picture us shivering there in the freezing cold for hours, waiting until the snow plows came to our rescue.

None of us were dressed for the storm, but

immediately Garth said, "Stay here. I won't be gone long."

He jumped out of the car and started walking through the woods—tromping through the semi-frozen snow with no coat or boots, just his tennis shoes.

When he arrived back, his arms were loaded with coats, gloves, hats and boots for me and the girls. We then walked home in cozy comfort.

Garth doesn't need to talk about the love he has for his family—he demonstrates it daily with his provision and protection.

10. Change yourself before attempting to change others.

I've heard wives say, "I'm praying he will change. Then everything will be alright."

In reality, the only effective prayer is, "Lord, make me a new person. Help me to become what You want me to be. Reveal what is not acceptable to You and show me what I can do that is pleasing to my husband."

Read God's Word. Allow scripture to point out the changes you need to make in both your thoughts and behavior. As you work on yourself, you will notice the situations around you will also be transformed. How is this possible? God is working *through* you. Suddenly you are a living epistle, demonstrating the fruit of the Spirit—*"love, joy, peace, patience, kindness, goodness, faithfulness, gentleness, self-control"* (Galatians 5:22-23).

What an impact those qualities will make—both in you and those you love.

Don't try to become a new person on your own. Ask for your Heavenly Father's help. *"And do not be conformed to this world, but be transformed by the renewing of your mind, so that you may prove what the will of God is, that which is good and acceptable and perfect"* (Romans 12:2).

11. Give preference to your husband.

We are living in a generation when pop psychologists have brainwashed women into believing the only questions worth asking are:

- "What can you do for me?"
- "How will this make me happy?"
- "What will I get out of the relationship?"

As a result, our homes are filled with self-centered wives whose only desire is to be pampered and catered to.

This is a far cry from Paul's admonition that we: *"Be devoted to one another in brotherly love; give preference to one another in honor"* (Romans 12:10).

What a change would take place in marriages if women began telling their husbands, "Honey, I love you. How can I help you?"

Don't think it is a one-way street. Before long, the

husband who is truly appreciated responds in kind—and begins to give his wife the love and attention she desperately longs for.

Remember, the marriage relationship represents the relationship between Christ and His bride, the church. He says if we keep His commandments, He will do whatever we ask. In the same way, if a woman truly pleases a man, he will do anything for her!

12. Make the Lord the head of your home.

In this book we have shared what the Bible says concerning the man being the head of the house. The ultimate leader, however, is the one who sets the home in order—God Himself.

As a wife and mother, my daily prayer has been for my husband, and children, to be raised in a family where the Lord is honored.

Again and again I opened the pages of my Bible and read these verses, which have been the foundation of my Christian walk: *"Trust in the Lord with all thine heart; and lean not unto thine own understanding. In all thy ways acknowledge him, and he shall direct thy paths"* (Proverbs 3:5-6 KJV).

Not only did Garth rededicate his life to Christ, thankfully, our two daughters are also serving the Lord. Julie is a capable Spirit-led leader who works with us at TCT and Vicki is in Tulsa where she and her husband are raising a wonderful Christian family.

Proverbs 13:22 says, *"...a good man leaves an*

inheritance to his children's children." Garth has done that for our seven grandchildren, Tommy, Natalie and Michael Nolan, and Lauren, Drew, Claire and Annabelle Clark.

Every day, I praise God for His faithfulness.

You, or someone you love, may be in a situation where your family does not live for the Lord. Begin to claim God's promise that your entire household will one day serve Christ.

The Lord desires for His children to live in a *"household of faith"* (Galatians 6:10 KJV).

When God used a great earthquake to deliver Paul and Silas from prison, their Philippian jailer cried, *"Sirs, what must I do to be saved?"* (Acts 18:30).

They told him, *"Believe in the Lord Jesus, and you will be saved, you and your household"* (v.31).

That same night, Paul and Silas spoke the word of the Lord to him and all who were in his home. The Bible records, *"immediately he was baptized, he and all his household"* (v.33).

Scripture also tells us how the Spirit spoke to Cornelius telling him Peter would come to his home and *"speak words to you by which you will be saved, you and all your household."* (Acts 11:13-14).

I believe this promise is also written for you.

A "PROVERBS 31" WOMAN

If you are curious to know the qualities of the "Ideal Woman," read the last chapter of the book of Proverbs.

King Solomon describes a wife of noble character who conducts herself with dignity and effectiveness in the marketplace, yet her first priority is her home life—making sure her family is well taken care of.

She rises early to prepare nutritious food for her household, manages her employees effectively and takes care of both spiritual and material concerns.

This competent, attractive woman knows what it means to succeed in life. Most important, she treats her husband with love and respect—and because of her positive attitude, he has great confidence in her. She cooperates with him and builds him up.

What is the result? He is honored and admired in the community because his wife represents him so well.

Here are the characteristics of the *Proverbs 31* woman. How many of these qualities do you possess?

- Trustworthy (v.10).
- Good (v.12).
- Faithful (v.12).
- Hard worker (v.13)
- Provider (v.14).
- Organized (v.15).
- Generous (v.15).
- Industrious (v.16).
- Strong (v.17).
- Has endurance (v.18).
- A homemaker (v.19).

- Charitable (v.20).
- Well prepared (v.21).
- A stylish dresser (v.22).
- Wife of a respected husband (v.23).
- A smart business woman (v.24).
- Dignified (v.25).
- Optimistic (v.25).
- Wise (v.26).
- Kind (v.26).
- A motivator (v.27).
- Esteemed by her family (v.28).
- High achiever (v.29).
- Fears the Lord (v.30).
- Productive (v.31).
- Praiseworthy (v.31).

Don't be overwhelmed by this long list. These are attributes to emulate—and with God's help you can.

Most meaningful to me are these words: *"Her children rise up and bless her; her husband also, and he praises her, saying: 'Many daughters have done nobly, But you excel them all'"* (Proverbs 31:28-29).

I am praying that as a result of putting these principles into action, your marriage will be richly blessed and your family will be embraced by God's love.

CHAPTER 8

CLEAR SKIES AHEAD

I am often asked, "What is the future of TCT?"

Garth and I want to continue broadcasting the Gospel until Jesus returns. We believe this ministry was birthed by the Spirit and what is born of God will remain and produce fruit (1 John 5:18).

A century ago it would have been impossible for people to conceive of Christian broadcasting. It is a unique media for this time period.

Technology is multiplying so rapidly we can hardly keep pace. We once heard the term "Renaissance Man"—a person of broad intellectual interests who knew practically everything about both the arts and science. With today's explosion of knowledge, such a person is virtually impossible to find.

The Bible says in *"the time of the end: many shall run to and fro, and knowledge shall be increased"* (Daniel 12:4 KJV). I believe we are living in that time.

At the speed the world is presently developing, if the Lord tarries, none of us can possibly conceive what communications will be like in the future.

A Person-to-Person Ministry

From my "right hand" vantage point, I marvel at what the Lord is doing. Today, TCT's television signal is available to over 30 million people in 15 states and Canada. We also take the Gospel to more than 100 million homes in 170 nations throughout the world via direct-to-home satellite—in Europe, Africa, Australia, Asia and the Middle East. In addition, TCT is also available to millions of cable homes in India and the Philippines.

Through our Internet website (www.tct.tv) we are able to stream video of our Christ-centered programs.

While the ministry is global in scope, we have always maintained a strong local foundation—and a commitment to build the body of Christ in the communities in which our stations are located.

Even though TCT is a broadcast outreach, it is also a person-to-person ministry through our Global Prayer Chain. Our Prayer Centers in the U.S. and Asia receive thousands of calls from people around the globe.

What began as the call of God to one, has now become the shared vision of many—reaching and touching souls with the life-changing message of Christ.

WHAT'S ON THE HORIZON?

I believe God raised up our ministry for this time and place in history. It is a tool to spread the Gospel to as many as possible in this generation.

Media gurus are predicting over-the-air television stations will soon be like dinosaurs—with satellite and other delivery systems taking their place. This is why we are listening for the Lord's guidance as we continue our mission to take the message to the ends of the earth. Garth is praying for discernment concerning what the Spirit is saying to the church today (Revelation 3:22).

Whatever the decision, he knows I will be by his side.

The Second Coming of Jesus Christ is imminent and prophecy is being fulfilled at a rapid pace. I believe the time is near and until that glorious day, we have a mandate to fulfill the Great Commission.

At this moment there are more people living on planet earth than have ever been alive in all of history—and God desires for them to know His Son.

CREATIVE FISHING

Our goal from day one has been to touch the lives of people—right where they live. Not every program appeals to all, but as a fisherman will tell you, "To catch different kinds of fish, you need to use a variety of bait."

To be honest, the type of music that reaches young people for the Gospel isn't something I like—it's much to noisy and raucous for my ears! Yet, thousands of teens who are clicking the TV remote, stop at TCT when they see a Christian band and receive the message of Christ.

On the other end of the spectrum, not everyone is interested in a fishing program, yet we have such a telecast for those who are. It, too, shares the Gospel.

Jesus says, *"Behold, I send you forth as sheep in the midst of wolves: be ye therefore wise as serpents, and harmless as doves"* (Matthew 10:16 KJV).

Our goal is to reach people in every creative way we can—to present God's Son in all aspects of His personality, which is infinite.

"THANK YOU"

Each day, I thank God for our staff, volunteers and prayer partners. They are such a vital part of this outreach.

I truly believe every person who has given to our ministry understands what it means to be sitting "in the right seat"—supporting, encouraging and praying.

I want to say a heartfelt "Thank you" to those who have responded to the urging of the Spirit and have financially undergirded this work. It could not continue without partners such as you.

Certainly there are individuals who have given large gifts—including the twin-engine airplane. Yet, we are just as grateful and thrilled when we receive a check for $10 from a grandmother on Social Security. It is as important as the first $10 gift we received at the start of TCT.

Together, we are all an integral part of what the Lord is doing.

WHAT WILL REMAIN?

One day soon, we pray we will hear God say, *"Well done, thou good and faithful servant: thou hast been faithful over a few things, I will make thee ruler over many things: enter thou into the joy of thy lord"* (Matthew 25:21 KJV).

When the rewards are given, our works will be *"revealed with fire, and the fire itself will test the quality of each man's work"* (1 Corinthians 3:13).

Only what is truly done for Christ will remain—this is the foundation of *"gold, silver* [and] *precious stones"* (v.12).

I believe you will receive a rich reward from the Lord for being a partner—whether your giving is little or much. The Lord will honor your sacrifice.

AT GOD'S RIGHT HAND

Perhaps you have read this book and are saying, "I wish this could be *my* life—to know my purpose and live out the destiny the Almighty has planned."

You can! It begins by establishing a personal relationship with God's Son and accepting Him as your Lord and Savior.

Jesus came to earth to be born as a Man, but He died on the cross for your sin. Just as important, He rose again and ascended to heaven.

Where is Jesus at this very moment? He is in the right seat, next to His Father—*"...the author and finisher of our faith; who for the joy that was set before him endured the cross, despising the shame, and is set down at the right hand of the throne of God"* (Hebrews 12:2 KJV).

A TRANSFORMATION

Nicodemus, a very educated man, came to Jesus one night. He knew the Lord performed miracles, yet he didn't understand the source of power.

Jesus declared to him, *"Truly, truly, I say to you, unless one is born again he cannot see the kingdom of God"* (John 3:3).

It takes the new birth experience to even *begin* to

perceive the spiritual realm. Without this, you are blinded to the things of God.

Nicodemus asked, *"How can a man be born when he is old? He cannot enter a second time into his mother's womb and be born, can he?"* (v.3).

The Lord explained that salvation is a spiritual transformation which occurs in your heart and mind—not a literal, physical rebirth.

This new beginning means making Christ the Lord of your life and seeking His will. When you have taken this step of faith, the Holy Spirit comes alongside as your comforter and guide—because Jesus promised He would send another Helper who would be with us *"forever"* (John 14:16). The Holy Spirit is available to lead you in making the right decisions and helping you understand the things of God as never before.

THE A, B, C'S

Jesus is ready to make intercession with the Father on your behalf. It's as easy as A, B, C:

> **A**ccept Him.
> **B**elieve Him.
> **C**onfess Him.

The Bible says, *"...if you confess with your mouth*

Jesus as Lord, and believe in your heart that God raised Him from the dead, you will be saved" (Romans 10:9).

This is the starting point for a spiritual journey which leads to an eternity in heaven.

YOUR PRAYER

If you have never accepted the Lord before, there is no better time than at this moment. Your life will change and the Lord will welcome you into His Kingdom.

Let me ask you to pray this prayer with me:

Father, in Jesus' name, I come to You and ask You to receive me.

Lord, I repent of my sin. Forgive me and cleanse my heart with the precious blood Your Son shed for me on the cross.

Holy Spirit, come and direct me in all things. Show me the path I should walk and lead me to those who will encourage and strengthen me.

I acknowledge Your Lordship from this moment and promise to read Your Word, pray every day, seek Your will and fellowship with believers.

I thank You for saving me now. In Jesus' name, Amen.

A TIME TO REMEMBER

Now that you have turned your life over to Christ, tell someone about your decision—perhaps a family friend, a relative who is already a Christian or a local pastor. Speaking your confession helps to seal it in your heart and makes it much easier to begin walking with the Lord.

Let me encourage you to call our Prayer Center, 313-534-1818, and have someone agree with you concerning your decision. A wonderful believer will share a few scriptures and help you get started on your new life in Christ. We would also love to send you some printed materials to encourage you along the way.

Why is this important? You need to have a point in time to remember, "Yes, that's when I accepted Christ."

As soon as possible, find a Bible-believing, Spirit-filled church with people who will help you grow in faith.

A NEW CIRCLE

Now that you are a member of God's family, share your faith, embrace the lonely and offer a hand to those who are tired and weak.

Even when people don't understand your decision to serve Christ, keep praying, keep believing and one day they will.

Years ago, I read these words which continue to speak to my heart. They were written by Edwin Markham, the nineteenth century poet:

> *They drew a circle that shut me out,*
> *Heretic, rebel, a thing to flout.*
> *But love and I had the wit to win,*
> *We drew a circle that took them in.*

Through Christ, God drew a circle that took us in, and we can do the same for others.

STILL FLYING!

It has been a long flight since the Lord gave Garth a vision for Christian televison in the 1970s.

Today, our old Cessna 310—the airplane that shuttled us back and forth between those first two stations—has long since been replaced by a newer Cessna 421. Garth still flies it himself, and I'm there with him in the right seat.

Day after day the skies become clearer as we keep sending the Gospel to as many lost souls as possible.

Thank you for joining with us on this exciting journey.

TO CONTACT THE AUTHOR
OR TO LEARN MORE ABOUT TCT:

TCT MINISTRIES
P.O. BOX 1010
MARION, IL 62959

PHONE: 618-997-9333
U.S. PRAYER CENTER: 313-534-1818
INTERNET: www.tct.tv
EMAIL: correspondence@tct.tv